Field to Flask

The Fundamentals of Small Batch Distilling

M. Bucholtz, B.Sc, MBA

Field to Flask

The Fundamentals of Small Batch Distilling

Wood Dragon Books

Box 1216, Regina, Saskatchewan, Canada, S4P 3B4

www.wooddragonbooks.com

ISBN #978-0-9948700-5-6

DISCLAIMER

References are made throughout this book to the notion of home distilling. Although home distilling is against the law in many jurisdictions, some locations have recently adopted a more relaxed stance towards small batch home distilling, provided it is for personal consumption only. The author and publisher of this book bear no responsibility whatsoever for readers of this book who run afoul of the law while distilling at home.

Cover Credits: Cover Image courtesy of Black Fox Distilling, Saskatoon, Saskatchewan, CANADA

ACKNOWLEDGMENTS

Special acknowledgement goes out to the Institute for Brewing & Distilling in London, England. I would not be teaching others about the art and science of distillation, I would not be consulting to start-up craft distillers, and I would not have written this book were it not for having successfully written your General Certificate in Distilling Exam that launched me on this most unusual trajectory in late 2014. Thank You! Cheers!

DEDICATION

This book is dedicated to all of you who enjoy spending time in your garages, back-yard sheds and man caves pursuing the art and science of fermentation and distillation. You know who you are. Keep up the good work.

This book is also dedicated to entrepreneurs who are thinking about starting a craft distillery or supplying goods and services to craft distillers. The craft distilling revolution is just beginning and already the corporate suits at the big commercial distillers are getting nervous. Welcome to the revolution. It's going to be a whole lot of fun!

CONTENTS

1

NOTE FROM THE AUTHOR

Cycles of nature fascinate me. Cycles of human behavior fascinate me. It is this fascination with cycles that somehow drew me into the realm of distilled spirits three years ago. I have been brewing beer, wine and mead at home for 30 years. A few years ago, I could sense that a cycle had made a bottom and was now gathering upward momentum. My curiosity was piqued.

In the early 1790s, American settlers took up arms when the government of the day tried to impose a Whisky Tax. Cooler heads eventually prevailed. Government backed down and people were allowed to make and enjoy their Whisky minus the heavy hand of the taxman. Some 120 years later, another cyclical point was hit when governments imposed Prohibition. People fought back. Some, like the Bronfman family from Saskatchewan, Canada and the Hatch brothers from Ontario, Canada made buckets of money moving booze to thirsty people. Governments eventually saw the light and the public was allowed to again enjoy alcohol legally.

We are again at what appears to be a cyclical point. Consumers are beginning to tire of the big corporate brand names and the slick corporate advertising campaigns. Consumers are now demanding different tasting distilled spirits made from unique and often locally grown raw materials. This time governments seem to have learned from the past and instead of standing in the way, are amending legislation and opening doors for small batch craft distilling. Granted, progress has been slower in some locales than in others, but progress it is nonetheless. There are now nearly 700 craft distillers licensed to do business in America. Canada has nearly 70 and the UK almost 100.

With my curiosity piqued, in early 2014, I enrolled to write a distilling exam through the UK-based Institute for Brewing & Distilling. It took me nearly nine months of reading and research to prepare for this exam. Early in my studies, I attended a 5-day Distilling Workshop in Gig Harbor, Washington put on by an outfit called the Artisan Craft Distilling Institute. I was profoundly disappointed at the lack of math, science and hands-on learning opportunities built in to this program. When I become disappointed, I tend to take swift action to make things right. Sitting in the classroom in Gig Harbor listening to some presenter drone on mindlessly about how to market with Facebook, I thought to myself - what if I were to establish a consulting organization in Canada to offer hands-on distillery courses to people interested in learning about the art and science of fermentation and distillation? What if I were to use my exam preparation materials as the basis for these courses? Some weeks later, by some peculiar quirk of fate, I found myself in the right place at the right time. During a business trip to Kelowna, British Columbia I ended up meeting Mr. Mike Urban, Master Distiller at Urban Distilleries. After listening to my idea for a properly designed 5-day Distilling Workshop, he suggested that we turn our sights to putting this idea into action at his distillery. We launched our first 5-day Workshop in October 2014 and have not looked back. This book you hold in your hands is the same material I regularly provide to participants in these Workshops. As of mid-2016 we have put over 200 people through our Workshops – some from as far away as Great Britain, Central America and South America. Many of these people have now ventured forth to start their own craft distilleries. Many others have forged ahead to simply become much better home distillers.

I now devote a big part of my energy to the craft distilling revolution. In addition to these 5-day Workshops, I spend considerable time working with start-up craft distilleries to help fine-tune business and marketing plans as well as recipe and mash bill formulations. Looking forward, I plan on expanding these Workshops across Canada so more people can gain knowledge of fermentation and distillation.

As a home brewer and home winemaker who long ago turned his back on the big brand names of beer and wine, it gives me great satisfaction to see the big commercial distillers getting increasingly more nervous as more and more craft distilled products show up on liquor store shelves. It thrills me to see people questing after knowledge of how Whisky, Gin and Vodka are made. I smile quietly to myself every time I hear of someone who has taken up the art of home distilling.

The distilled spirits landscape is being indelibly altered by small craft distillers. I am determined to play a part in changing this landscape through workshops, consultations to start-up craft distillers, research and more books on the subject.

Welcome to distilled spirits the way distilled spirits should taste.

Welcome to the craft distilling revolution.

2

A BRIEF HISTORY OF ALCOHOL

PHOENICIANS, GREEKS & ROMANS

The very earliest history of alcohol goes back to 5000 BC to an area of the world that today includes the lands bordered by the Black Sea and Caspian Sea. (Think modern-day Georgia, Azerbaijan, Armenia, Turkey and Iran). The humble apple and grape trace their lineage to this time and geographic region as well. The hunter-gatherer inhabitants of these ancient lands enjoyed eating the flesh of these fruits and drinking the juices squeezed from these fruits. One day, probably by accident, somebody left some crushed apples or grapes in an earthenware vessel. Bubbles began to form on the fruit and a gentle hissing sound could be heard coming from the vessel. Although not immediately understood in detail at the time, this was fermentation. After several days, when the juice from the earthenware container was sampled, a most peculiar observation was made. The juice now imparted a mild feeling of happiness to all those who sampled it.

Intoxication and its pleasant effects had been discovered.

Man is a curious creature and this curiosity gradually led to a deeper look at the intoxicating effects of fermented beverages. It was observed that if one took some fermented liquid in an earthenware vessel and gently heated the vessel, vapors could be seen rising from the vessel. Someone, somewhere eventually had the notion to take an animal skin and place it above the heated vessel to absorb and capture the rising vapors. Squeezing the captured liquid from the animal skin and drinking it yielded a startling observation. The pleasant feeling of happiness and euphoria was intensified.

The concentration of alcohol through distillation had been discovered.

Over the ensuing centuries, as hunter-gatherer man increased in number, he began to extend his reach into surrounding regions. He took with him the seeds of the apple and the grape. By 1200 BC, civilization had spread as far south as the Mediterranean Sea. The dominant civilization was the Phoenicians who lived in a series of city states called Tyre, Sidon and Biblos. Modern day Cyprus, Sardinia and Sicily also owe their existence to the Phoenicians.

As well as being skilled artisans and seafarers, the Phoenicians were accomplished at wine making and simple distillation. The Phoenician tongue had an expression for distilled alcoholic spirits which roughly translated into *water of life*. The Phoenicians travelled through modern day Spain, France and even as far north as Ireland and Scotland taking with them their knowledge of producing and distilling alcoholic beverages. The Phoenician expression *water of life* remains with us to this day in the Spanish *agua de ardiente*, the French *eau de vie* and the Gaelic *usque beatha.*

Rivalling the strength of the Phoenician civilization was the power and reach of the Greek civilization. The ancient Greeks ascribed sacred powers to distilled beverages and incorporated distilled spirits into religious ritual.

This ancient Greek knowledge of distillation remains with us to this day. Grape pomace (skin and pulp) and wine are distilled to make a spirit beverage called *Zivania.* Grape pomace is distilled to make *Tsipouro* and *Tsikoudia.* An anise infused version of these spirits remains with us today in the form of *Ouzo.*

By 200 BC, the Phoenician empire had collapsed with the Roman empire usurping the former glory of Phoenicia. By 150 BC, the Greek empire had too faded into the hands of the Romans. We know the Romans were involved in distillation for the Latin expression *de-stillare*, meaning to drip or trickle down, is the root of our modern English word *distillation.*

For the next several hundred years the Roman empire ruled supreme. But, like so many empires before it, the Roman empire eventually collapsed. Starting in 400 AD, the world as it existed at that time, lapsed into a period of negligible advancement called the Dark Ages. However, the knowledge that mankind had accumulated too date concerning the art and science of distillation was not to be lost.

ARABIAN SCIENCE

In or around 620 AD, a powerful new civilization emerged from the sandy deserts of Arabia. The Arabs were an aggressive lot and soon fanned out across the lands formerly ruled by Phoenicia, Rome and Greece. But, unlike civilizations before them who quested for power, the Arabs were on a quest for something different. They were on a mission to gather scientific and mathematical knowledge.

The Arabs gathered the fragmented knowledge of distillation from the former Roman, Greek and Phoenician civilizations and organized it into a clearer pattern. They made improvements to the crude containers and vessels these previous civilizations had used to distill beverages. The Arabs spread the knowledge of these improvements in still design along with knowledge of distillation into what is now modern day Spain, Portugal and France.

This Arab knowledge is with us yet today in the form of the al-Ambic still. Travel to France, Spain and Portugal and you will see distilled spirits artisans plying their craft using the Al-Ambic still design as illustrated in Figure 1.

Figure 1 al-Ambic Still

A typical al-Ambic still consists of a copper pot with an onion-shaped dome mounted on top. Alcoholic vapors flow through the gooseneck-like tube and into a water-cooled condenser

LE COGNAC

By 1300 AD, elite French families had started using the Al-Ambic design of still to create a beverage from grape juices. Today we recognize this distilled beverage as *Cognac.* The Spanish too started using this still design to make spirits. Today, many excellent brandies come from Spain including variations like *Licor de Orujo*, a pomace based brandy from northern Spain.

The production of Cognac is tightly regulated. The white wine distilled to make Cognac comprises 95% Ugni Blanc with the remainder being Folle Blanche and French Colombard. Cognac can only be produced in the Cognac region of France. This region in the western part of the country comprises the areas of Charente-Maritime and Charente. Within this geographic swath are six defined regions that attest to the quality of Cognac produced therein. At the top of this designation list is the Grand Champagne region. Bringing up the bottom of the list is Bois Ordinaire.

Cognac is also tightly regulated as to aging and production. It must be distilled twice in traditional copper stills, and then aged a minimum 30 months in French oak sourced from the Limousin and Troncais regions of central France. The aging process involves the use of new oak barrels, medium aged barrels and very old barrels – each being in contact with the aging spirit for prescribed intervals of time. Distillers may only produce Cognac between November 1 and March 31 following the grape harvest.

VODA

The knowledge of distilling eventually found its way to modern day Poland and Russia. By the 1500s, even the common man in these places had learned the art of distillation. In the 1600s, Peter the Great and later Catherine the Great embraced *Vodka*, or as it was called then, *Voda* – meaning water.

In 1818, with Vodka still strongly in fashion in Russia, Ivan Smirnov founded a company to distill Vodka. By 1886, his nephew Pyotr Smirnov had taken the reigns at the company. Pyotr, however, wanted to set the company apart from the other Vodka makers. He travelled to Europe and purchased a Coffey Still from Anneas Coffey. This design of still was a radical departure from the traditional pot stills of the era. The design was based on two columns and the resulting distillate was much cleaner that anything produced in a pot still. So good was the resulting Vodka that Czar Nicholas III formally endorsed Smirnov Vodka and set in motion its future success.

Pyotr died in 1898 and his son Vladimir took over the company. Corporate success, however, came to a sudden halt in 1917 with the Bolshevik Revolution which heralded the introduction of Communist rule. In quick order, the Communist Government seized Smirnov's assets and Vladimir fled the country with just the shirt on his back. After settling in France, he tried to re-establish the Smirnov brand but the French wanted nothing to do with this clear spirit, opting instead for their much loved brandies, Cognacs and Armagnacs. In 1934, with his health failing, Vladimir sold the worldwide rights and trademarks for Smirnov Vodka to a fellow Russian political refugee Rudolph Kunett for 54,000 Francs ($45,000 US dollars). Kunett set up shop in his adopted country of America in the small town of Bethel, Connecticut. But, Kunett soon ran into the same problem that had plagued Smirnov in France. Nobody wanted this clear spirit called Vodka. Americans at the time were enjoying their Whisky and bartenders in many cities were in favor of Gin cocktails. In 1939 Kunett admitted defeat and sold the Smirnov trademarks and rights to food and drink distributor G.F. Hublein Company for $14,000 US dollars plus a small per-bottle royalty.

Had Kunett held on for just one more year, his fortunes would have changed. World War II saw men head off to the battlefields and women take up jobs in the munitions factories. After a hard day in the factory, women wanted to relax with a drink at their local bar. But, they did not want harsh tasting Whisky. Bartenders were quick to realize that Vodka was the answer. Colorless and odorless, it would not corrupt the flavor of a drink made with juices or sodas.

The Vodka cocktail revolution was born. Bloody Mary's, Screwdrivers, and Moscow Mules were soon all the rage.

In the 1970s, the Swedish Government was in dire need of money and began looking for products it could sell on the world market. The Swedes were quick to realize that they had an asset in the form of a government owned company, Absolut Rent Branvin. The English translation of this name aptly says what this company made – Absolute Pure Vodka.

After granting creative freedom to ad agencies in New York, the Swedes launched *Absolut Vodka* in 1979. With clever artwork playing on the name 'Absolut' and on the unique bottle shape, this upstart new brand soon was catching serious attention from consumers. The big corporate spirits makers took notice too. In 2008, drinks giant Pernod Ricard bought the exclusive rights to *Absolut Vodka* for a cool $8.3 billion. *Absolut Vodka*, made from winter Wheat, continues to thrive as a brand name to this day. But recent data shows that sales, although still robust, are tapering off as the consumer continues to be presented with innovative Vodka product offerings from the craft distilling movement.

Dutch distilling concern, Nolet, also took notice of the Absolut brand success. In 1983, Nolet launched its *Ketel One Vodka* onto the world stage. Nolet took a more laid back approach with *Ketel One.* No glitzy ads from high powered agencies in New York. Just a clean, smooth Vodka that is a pleasure to sip neat. In 2008, drinks giant Diageo paid Nolet $1 billion for a 50% interest in the brand name. Many people ask me what Vodka I seek out at bars when I travel. The answer is: I sip *Ketel One Vodka* straight up at room temperature. In my not so humble opinion, the taste profile of *Ketel One* is what craft distillers should be aspiring to rival.

In 1996, American entrepreneur Sydney Frank decided to launch a Vodka. Capitalizing on 30 years of experience working with his father-in-law in the liquor distribution business, Frank knew what to do and where to turn. He quickly concluded that consumers would pay a premium for food or drinks that were from France. Frank turned to a commercial contract distiller in France and asked them to concoct a mash bill of Rye, Wheat, Barley and Corn. He decided that a frosted glass bottle bearing the colors of the French flag would be sure to grab the attention of the consumer. He further opted for a bottle that was slightly taller in the neck than competitor's bottles. Taller in the neck and frosted grey. Sounds like a goose, doesn't it? How about Grey Goose? Being a clever marketer, Frank took matters one step further. He retained the Beverage Tasting Institute to conduct a blind tasting of 40 different Vodkas from around the globe. Frank agreed to cover all the costs of this exercise. Not surprisingly, *Grey Goose* was awarded a composite score of 96/100. With that one data point in his pocket, he began proclaiming *Grey Goose* to be the world's best Vodka. Apparently people were paying attention. In 2004, Bacardi paid Frank $2.4 billion for the *Grey Goose* brand name.

THE RISE OF RUM

The 1500s heralded an age of global commerce unlike anything seen before. The Portuguese, being skilled mariners, soon found their way around the tip of Africa and onwards to India and as far as the Spice Islands of modern day Indonesia. One plant that was collected from these seagoing ventures was the sugar cane.

The sugar cane plant is native to modern day New Guinea. By 325 BC, the sugar cane plant had been brought to India where it flourished. The army of Alexander the Great passing through India called the sugar cane *honey from reeds.* Arab invaders circa 620 AD called the plant *sukkur*, from whence our modern word sugar is derived. Before long, this weed-like species found its way across the Atlantic ocean on Portuguese vessels where it quickly took root in the Caribbean islands.

History suggests that the first island to start growing cane was

Barbados. The islanders followed the old methods of the east Indian sugar merchants and began cooking the juice obtained from the sugar cane to produce crystals of sugar. The remaining sludge left over from the sugar extraction process – molasses – also proved of value, for the islanders understood the basic science of fermentation and distillation. Allowing the molasses sludge to ferment and then distilling the resulting alcoholic liquid produced a product that is consumed the world over to this day – *Rum.*

As trading vessels from Europe continued on to the American colonies, they often landed in places like Boston laden with barrels of molasses. Settlers began distilling copious amounts of Rum, or as it was often called in those days *kill-devil* or *rhum-bullion.* By 1661, Rum had become so commonplace that a court in Boston declared it to be a menace to society.

But, Rum was not to be defeated. In 1688, William of Orange who was sitting on the British Throne banned the import of French brandy, making Rum imported from the American colonies a hot commodity. Before long, even the British Navy adopted Rum and began distributing daily rations called *tots* to its sailors.

Between 1754 and 1763, the Seven Years War saw alliances between European nations severely tested and fought over. During this tumultuous period of world history, Britain occupied Cuba. With this occupation came the knowledge of sugar cane growing and Rum making. By 1799, Cuba was exporting two million gallons of molasses and 1.2 million gallons of Rum from a reported 300 small distilleries.

In the early 1800s, a Spanish businessman Don Facundo Bacardi Masso found his way to Cuba where he became a reasonably successful merchant. He eventually started dabbling in the art of making Rum, employing techniques like charcoal filtration and barrel aging to make the drink more palatable to the consumer in Europe.

By the late-1800s, his company was a flourishing success and its distilled product highly sought after in Europe. Today, Bacardi is a global force in the production of Rum and owns many other brands of spirit beverages including Bombay Sapphire Gin.

WHISKY TAX & BOURBON

The early 1600s saw the start of what would be many waves of migration to the New World. The brave settlers coming from afar brought with them their domestic grains. The Dutch and Germans brought rye grain. The English brought Barley and Wheat. It was soon discovered that these grains were capable of growing in the fertile soils of the New World. These hardy souls brought with them more than just grain. They brought their brewing and distilling equipment as well. This equipment consisted of likely nothing more than crude metal pots and wooden barrels. Rudimentary to be sure. But very effective nonetheless. Before long, beer and distilled alcohol were being made from the surplus grains remaining from the autumn harvests.

Brewing and distilling surged in popularity on into the mid-1700s. In 1789, newly elected President George Washington found himself leading a nation in deeply in debt. Some $54 million had been borrowed from France to finance the War of Independence. To pay this debt back, Washington and his Treasury Secretary Alexander Hamilton imposed a Whisky Tax on the settlers. So vigorous was the backlash, that by 1802 the tax had been repealed. Many settlers in the wake of this disastrous attempt to tax Whisky headed west into present day Kentucky and Tennessee to get away from the reach of the Government. This wave of migration westward is what set the stage for the modern day Kentucky Bourbon and Tennessee Whisky industries. The names of many of these settlers are with us yet today. Elijah Pepper (Old Crow Bourbon), Jacob Beam (Jim Beam brands), Robert Samuels (Maker's Mark Bourbon) and Basil Hayden

(Basil Hayden's Bourbon) to name a few.

GENEVER & GIN

By the early 1600s, the Dutch had already been distilling alcohol of modest quality and blending it with Barley wine. In 1602 the Dutch East India Company was formed and soon began sailing the route to the Spice Islands in search of exotic spices much like the Portuguese had done decades earlier. Today, we recognize this geographic area as the islands in the Indonesian archipelago. A spice called Juniper soon found its way into Dutch distilled alcohol and the new creation was a product called Genever.

In 1638, in England, Charles I granted exclusivity on grain distilled spirits production for a 21 mile radius around London to his political friends at the Worshipful Company of Distillers. Politics entered into the fray again in 1689 when James I was driven from the throne. English parliament turned to Holland for help and asked William of Orange (who was married to Mary – daughter of James I) to assume the English throne under the title William III. Dutch Genever soon found its way into English social circles along with grain alcohol from the 21 mile radius around London. What emerged from this unlikely combination was a product called Gin.

England was at odds with Louis XIV of France and so to destroy demand for French brandy, William III enacted legislation to allow essentially anyone to distill grain spirit. The excise duties collected on this increased volume of spirits production further helped finance the conflict with France. In a further bid for funds, the English Parliament imposed steeper duties on beer. This in turn led to even more people taking to Gin. For the next 50 years, Gin consumption continued to grow, but so did the attendant social problems. As quickly as government enacted legislation to curb the legal production of Gin, illicit distillers sprang into action to feed demand.

Things got so bad that Gin came to be known as *Mother's Ruin* – a reference to its dire effects on the health of new born babies. It took a crop failure in 1757 to finally counter the Gin problem. On the heels of this failed harvest, a temporary ban was imposed on all grain distillation. Sobriety quickly returned to the streets of London as people stopped to reflect on the evils of Gin.

In 1760, distillation was again approved, but at much higher excise rates. With the benefits of sobriety now appreciated and with a growing moral movement providing added impetus, Gin production was soon restored but with a new respect for moderate consumption. The next hundred years would see the creation of many Gin producers, the names of whom are still with us today, such as Tanqueray, Gordon's, Boodles, Beefeater and Gilbey's, to name a few.

As the 1800s neared an end, Gin found its way to America and into cocktails. The Gin cocktail movement continued right into the 1900s with World War I even failing to put a dent in consumption. Drinks like the Ramos Gin Fizz, Pink Lady, the Negroni and the Singapore Sling became wildly popular.

Today, the Gin movement remains strong and with craft distillers now leading the charge, I have no doubt that Gin will remain a popular spirit for a long time to come.

CANADIAN ENTREPRENEURS & PROHIBITION

To complete this brief look at the history of alcohol, let us now circle back to the late 1700s and the waves of immigration that were landing on the shores of Upper and Lower Canada.

In 1783, the Molson family arrived from England and settled in Montreal. John Molson soon opened a brewery in Montreal and the seeds for the future success of the Molson's Beer brand were planted. During one of his return visits to England, Molson acquired a couple of copper pot stills. In about 1820, his eldest son Thomas Molson began distilling Whisky. At this time there were an estimated 70 distilleries located up and down the St. Lawrence River, all producing product for export back to a thirsty English marketplace.

By 1845, however, this market dried up and many of these small distilleries faded into memory. In 1867, the year Canada became a country, the Molson family made the decision to finally exit the spirits business and concentrate full time on beer. The next time you are enjoying a cold glass of Molson Canadian beer, remember that the Molson family was not always just about beer.

In 1832, a pair of English immigrants, James Worts and his brother in-law William Gooderham, arrived in Toronto and soon set up a grain milling operation. In 1845, looking to expand their business, they decided to venture into the production of Whisky using a mash made of Wheat. Their timing was otherwise perfect as the American Civil War that had erupted in 1859 wreaked havoc on the many distilleries that dotted the landscape from New York to the Carolinas. Gooderham and Worts seized the opportunity and by late 1860 were making 2.5 million gallons of Whisky a year, much of it destined for a thirsty America. Gooderham and Worts were unwavering British imperialists. In 1916, after having amassed huge wealth from making Whisky, they decided to idle their production facility in Toronto as a show of support for the efforts of Britain in World War I. In 1923, upstart Whisky entrepreneur Harry Hatch purchased their Toronto facility for $1.5 million.

One very colorful figure who left his mark on Canadian Whisky was American-born Hiram Walker. Walker was born in Massachusetts in 1816. In 1846, he landed in Detroit where he set up shop providing dry goods to settlers heading west. He also began experimenting with rectification. In those days, a rectifier was one who purchased raw alcohol distillate from a larger distiller. This raw distillate was then charcoal filtered and doctored with caramel burnt sugar and prune juice to make a palatable spirit drink. When US Laws changed and rectifiers came under duress, Walker scarcely blinked. He packed up his equipment and headed across the border to present day Windsor, Ontario. In 1858, with assistance from his brother Harrington, he set up shop making Whisky from a mash of what is reported to be 80% Corn, 14% Rye, 3% Barley and 3% Oats. This recipe was the forerunner of a brand of spirit drink that remains very popular to this day – *Canadian Club Whisky*.

In 1926, the Canadian government struck a committee (the Smuggling Committee) to investigate how distillers had managed to evade paying Excise Tax during the Prohibition years. What was revealed was a complex web of corruption that involved distillers and senior level bureaucrats. With the Volstead Act still in force in America, Hiram Walker realized that as an American citizen he faced possible incarceration in America if he were ever called to testify under oath in front of the Canadian government's Smuggling Committee. In December 1926, a hurried deal was consummated that saw Harry Hatch purchase the assets of the Hiram Walker Distillery for $14 million. No longer associated with the distillery, Walker was no longer under any duress to appear before any government committees.

Two massive acquisitions were made inside of three years. Who was this Harry Hatch? The Hatch family was already in the liquor business when Harry was born in 1884 near Belleville, Ontario. As a young man, alongside with his brother Herb, he worked in various bars and hotels in the area. In 1911, he set out on his own and established a package liquor store in Whitby, Ontario. Success followed and two years later Hatch moved his business into downtown Toronto. In 1916, when the Ontario government ushered in the Ontario Temperance Act, Harry and his brother barely blinked. They packed up shop and re-located to Montreal where they established a mail-order business selling Whisky to their former clients in Toronto and surrounding area. Hatch's success soon attracted the attention of Montreal businessman Sir Mortimer Davis, head of both the Canadian Industrial Alcohol Company and Imperial Tobacco. The Volstead Act in America had created a thirsty marketplace. Harry Hatch partnered with Davis and wasted little time in assembling a fleet of motor boats. By 1923, 50,000 gallons of Whisky a month was finding its way by boat across Lake Ontario into upstate New York. Harry Hatch had become a very wealthy man. Mortimer Davis became even more wealthy than he already had been.

In 1825, John P. Wiser was born in Utica, New York into a family of successful industrialists. The family eventually established a distillery in Prescott, Ontario and young J.P. was put in charge of operations. His mash bill apparently was based on Corn and Rye – but with a twist. Wiser also added hops to his Whisky. By the early 1900s, Wiser was exporting his product around the world. Whisky historians suggest that Wiser's may have been the first Whisky brand to label itself as a 'Canadian Whisky'. In 1911, J.P. Wiser died. His children lacked the interest to continue running the business. Company Treasurer, Albert Whitney, took over running the operation, but in 1927 he passed away too. The Wiser's Distillery and brand name were then acquired by Montreal businessman Sir Mortimer Davis.

It is fascinating that history records *Wiser's Red Letter Rye* from the early 1900s as being 'dark in color and smooth'. In late 2015, the J.P. Wiser brand launched its *Wiser's Hopped Whisky*. With its dark color and smoothness, this is a page taken right out of the corporate history book. I further suspect this move is to try and counter the success of the growing craft distilling movement.
In 1837, the Seagram family arrived from England and settled near

Toronto in the town of Galt. Octavius Seagram and his wife had two boys, Joseph and Edward. Young Joseph proved quite talented with pencil and paper and in 1864 the Waterloo Distilling Company hired him to be their bookkeeper. Some 20 years later, he engineered a deal to buy out the company which he re-named the Joseph E. Seagram Distilling Company. Annual production was nearly one million gallons a year. His secret to success was apparently aging his Whisky in ex-sherry casks for four years.

Social pressures, however, were mounting. The evils of alcohol were coming under scrutiny and politicians were under pressure to act. Politicians were also feeling pressure from the large distillers who had been donating money to them to fund re-election campaigns. In 1883, with large distillers feeling the pinch of softening sales, the Canadian government returned the favor and passed the *Bottled In Bond Law* which stipulated that no taxes would be owing on Whisky until such time as it had been bottled and sold. In 1885, the Canadian government went one step further with amended legislation stating that Whisky had to be aged two years in order to be formally be called a Whisky. This proved disastrous to the many small distillers who relied on quick product turnover to generate cash flow. But, this legislation proved fortuitous to the large distillers. As the small distillers faded out of business, politicians argued that the evils of alcohol were being kept in check. As the small distillers faded away, the large distillers quietly solidified their grip on the spirits industry. Start-up craft distillers today should remain ever mindful of this symbiotic relationship between Government and the big commercial distillers. This relationship still quietly exists and could rear its ugly head at any time.

In 1898, with social pressures continuing to mount, the government of Prime Minister Wilfred Laurier made provision for a national referendum on the subject of implementing a prohibition ban on alcohol. History shows that 51.3% of people voted in favor of banning alcohol. But, Laurier, ever the clever and calculating politician, decided not to impose a ban on alcohol after seeing that only 44% of eligible voters had cast a ballot.

Prohibition did eventually come to Canada between 1901 and 1921. Prince Edward Island was the first province to implement a prohibition ban on alcohol in 1901. Ontario and Alberta followed in 1916. Saskatchewan, British Columbia and New Brunswick followed in 1917. Nova Scotia was the last to ban alcohol in 1921. Quebec, interestingly enough, adopted a prohibition ban on alcohol in 1919, but repealed the ban some two months later.

One of the most fascinating families in the history of alcohol in Canada – the Bronfman family – are synonymous with the prohibition of alcohol. The Bronfman family arrived in tiny Yorkton, Saskatchewan in 1889 with three children in tow – Abe, Harry and Sam. Four daughters were eventually born into the family as well. This family was entrepreneurial in every sense of the word. If there was a dollar to be made – whether selling horses, running hotels or selling cars, they figured out a way to make that dollar.

In 1919, the Canadian government passed the Canada Temperance Act. Those lobbying in favor of this Act were certain it would be damning to the alcohol trade. But, the government of the day was clever and on the lookout for its big distiller friends. The Act stated that it would be illegal to ship alcohol into any province, but only if that province first held a referendum to ratify the Canada Temperance Act. Individual provinces were not interested in having referendums.

With the news that the Temperance Act lacked any teeth, the Bronfman family swung into action, setting up a booze mail order business. Consumers across the country with money and means could now obtain a bottle of Whisky through the mail.

In 1917, the Canadian government moved to squash the booze mail order business. But, the Bronfmans were not deterred. World War I had created a huge surplus of Whisky in Scotland. The Bronfmans quickly figured out that it was still legal for a person to obtain Whisky by way of a doctor's note. The Canada Pure Drug Company was set up and it began importing boat loads of Scotch Grain Whisky into the port of Montreal. From there, the Canadian Pacific Railroad transported carloads of it to Yorkton, Saskatchewan into the waiting arms of the then twenty-eight year old Sam Bronfman.

Sam worked up to 22 hours some days charcoal filtering the Whisky and adjusting the flavor with caramel and prune juice. A typical blend consisted of 100 gallons of aged Rye Whisky, 318 gallons of 65% alcohol and 382 gallons of water.. Forged labels bearing names such as Gold Label and Special Vat Whisky were then applied. Before long, the Canada Pure Drug Company became the supplier of choice to medical practices and retail druggists across the Prairie provinces and into Ontario earning a reported $390,000 a month in gross revenues.

But, the Canada Pure Drug Company needed bonded warehouses to properly distribute its merchandise. Excise Canada bent the rules, looked the other way and allowed the Bronfman family to build a series of warehouses from Ontario to British Columbia. These facilities soon became known as 'boozoriums'. History shows that there were at least 25 of these facilities in Saskatchewan alone.

From Yorkton, some of the Canada Pure Drug Company merchandise found its way south to Moose Jaw, Saskatchewan thanks to a handshake deal that Harry and Sam Bronfman had made with a mysterious figure in a wheat field near the village of Bienfait, Saskatchewan. That mysterious figure was none other than Chicago gangster Al Capone. Moose Jaw was the terminus for the Soo Line

Railroad which ran down through Estevan, Saskatchewan on into Fargo, North Dakota and eventually into Chicago. No exact figures are available, but there is no doubt that a goodly amount of product found its way from Moose Jaw into Al Capone's hands and then into the thirsty American market.

As an aside to this story, in late 2015 I was at Prichard's, a small craft distillery just outside Nashville, Tennessee. Apparently the exploits of the Bronfman family are still talked about in America. When a couple of gentleman at the tasting bar realized that I was Canadian, their first comments were to the effect that "ya'll up there in Canada made a lot of money supplying America with Whisky during Prohibition". Indeed we did and there are many colorful figures, including the Bronfman clan, who shall be remembered in the history books as having played leading roles.

As Prohibition wound down and society came to again accept alcohol, the Bronfman family bought a distillery in Kentucky. They disassembled it piece by piece and moved it to Montreal where they set up shop as legalized distillers under the corporate banner Distillers Corporation Limited. Their success continued with the purchase of Joseph E. Seagram Distilling Company in 1928. By 1971, the Bronfman empire had grown to include some 39 distilleries worldwide. Sadly, the Bronfman empire eventually faltered under the watch of Edgar Jr. – the 3rd generation of the family. Today drinks giant Diageo owns the spoils of this former grand empire.

The post-Prohibition era was also profitable for Mortimer Davis and Harry Hatch. The distilling assets that made this duo so much money were folded into a legalized entity called Consolidated Distillers Ltd. Today, global spirits heavyweight Pernod Ricard owns this former success story.

THE LURE OF HISTORY

I could continue on for many more pages detailing the history of Canadian Whisky. Instead, I refer you to the very excellent treatment of the subject by author and esteemed Whisky expert Davin deKergommeaux in his book aptly entitled *Canadian Whisky, The Portable Expert.* You will find this book for sale on-line and in your local bookstore. I have even seen it being retailed in some liquor stores.

My travels and observations over the past several years have shown that the consumer is fascinated with the history of alcohol. Nowhere was this more apparent to me than in late 2015 in Paducah, Kentucky – the home of the Moonshine Company. Stepping inside this craft distillery was like taking a step back in time. The entire front part of this craft distillery is a veritable museum dedicated to that iconic spirit, *Moonshine.* From the collection of old stills, old posters and old photographs, there was something for everyone. By the time visitors reached the tasting bar, their emotions were so stoked they could hardly wait to make a purchase.

If you are intent on building a small craft distillery, incorporate history into your marketing efforts. Search out old stills, photographs and posters from bygone eras. Do what the big commercial distillers are not doing. Make your distillery and your products a complete emotional experience for the customer.

REFERENCES

Rum – A Social and Sociable History of the Real Spirit of 1776, Ian Williams, 2005, Nation Books, USA.

Vodka – Discovering, Exploring, Enjoying, Ian Wisniewski, 2003, Ryland,

Peters & Small, USA.

Vodka Classified, Stuart Walton, 2009, Anova Books, UK.

Big Shots - The Men Behind the Booze, A.J. Blaine, 2003, Penguin Books, USA.

Bourbon Whisky – Our Native Spirit, Bernie Lubbers, 2011, Blue River Press, USA.

Difford's Guide – Gin, Simon Difford, 2013, Firefly Books, USA.

Vodka – How a Colorless, Odorless, Flavorless Spirit Conquered America, V. Matus, 2014, Globe Pequot Press, USA.

Canadian Whisky, The Portable Expert, D. deKergommeaux, 2012, Ancient Forest Friendly Publishing, Canada.

The Early History of Distillation, T. Fairley, Proceedings of the 1907 Annual Meeting, Journal of the Institute of Brewing, Volume 13, Issue 6, pages 559–582, November-December 1907.

Booze – The Impact of Whisky on the Prairie West, James Gray, 1972, Macmillan Company of Canada.

Booze, Boats and Billions, C.W. Hunt, 1988, McLelland & Stewart.

3

SPIRITS DEFINITIONS

As a craft distiller, the products you can and cannot make are tightly regulated by government. It is prudent to follow these definitions at all times. Getting caught deviating from them can have dire consequences for the future viability of your business.

CANADA

The following are the alcoholic spirit definitions in Canada as prescribed by the Consolidated Regulations of Canada, section 870 (crc 870):

Grain Spirit: in Canada a craft distiller can make a mash of cereal grains (ie Wheat, Corn, Rye, Barley, Oats etc..) and ferment that mash with yeast to produce alcohol. Distilling the fermented mash to a sufficiently high proof that all or nearly all of the naturally occurring substances have been removed will then allow you to call the product a Grain Spirit. In reality, what a Grain Spirit will be is an alcoholic distillate that will have a slight grainy profile on the palate. Not something the consumer will want to sip straight up. Rather, a Grain Spirit will be something the consumer will want to consume as a mixed drink. One craft distiller that is making headway with a Grain Spirit is the Toronto Distilling Company. I have never had the pleasure of sipping this product, but I have heard favorable comments from many people.

Vodka: the strict definition of a Vodka says that it is a potable alcoholic spirit obtained by treating a Grain Spirit or Potato Spirit with charcoal so as to render it without distinctive character, aroma or taste. In reality, a craft distiller will end up initially distilling a grain mash into a Grain Spirit and then re-distilling that product again.

Following the second distillation, the distillate will either be exposed to granulated charcoal and then filtered through a plate filter or run through a filter device equipped with charcoal cartridges.

Despite the words in this definition calling for no distinctive taste or aroma, many of the Vodkas made by the large commercial distillers will still have some aroma or taste to them. In the many workshops I have conducted, participants without fail will always spot the rubbing alcohol aromas in Smirnoff Vodka. They will likewise pick up the less than desirable subtleties in both Grey Goose and Absolut Vodkas.

There is a significant opportunity at hand for craft distillers to produce a clean Vodka that feels pleasant on the tongue and that has one's taste-buds calling for more. My research has shown that at the time in Russian history when Pyotr Smirnov was producing his much loved Vodka, it was common practice to drink Vodka straight-up at room temperature in small quantities while dining. It is lamentable that today when the consumer sees Vodka, he or she instinctively reaches for something to mix with it. I believe with some encouragement and education, the consumer can be convinced to start enjoying Vodka straight up, in small quantities much as one would enjoy a wee dram of single malt Scotch.

A craft distiller may want to give thought to producing a couple different Vodkas. Perhaps a lighter profile version with Wheat, a spicier version with Rye grain and a sweet, creamy version with Triticale grain.

The definition of Vodka makes a further reference to Potato Spirit. I am aware of only a couple craft distilleries in Canada that are making spirits with potato. One is Yukon Shine Distillery in Whitehorse, Yukon who use a mix of Yukon Gold potato and Rye grain. The other is Schramm's Distillery in Pemberton, British Columbia. Potato as a raw material can be challenging to work with. In my Distillery

Workshops I used to provide taste samples of the Schramm's product. Without fail, people spotted what they described as an earthy, garden-like aroma. This was likely due to inadequate distilling and inadequate charcoal filtering. In early 2016, Schramm's product was de-listed from Government Liquor Stores in British Columbia due to lagging sales. Based on the observations in the Workshops, I think I know why sales were lacking.

One question that often comes up in my workshops concerns the distillation of surplus wine to make Vodka. According to the strict definition, a distiller cannot assign the name Vodka to a distillate made from wine, because wine is obviously not a cereal grain. However, distilling wine will generate a distillate of ethanol which is in alignment with section B.02.002 of the crc 870 regulations. Hence, it is possible to make a Vodka-like product from wine and call it something else. For example, the Diageo-owned brand *Ciroc* sells in Canada as a Spirit Drink. Dillons Distilling in Ontario, Canada simply calls their *Method 95* product a Liquor, even though one will find it on liquor stores shelves in the Vodka section. If you have never tried either of these products, I suggest doing so. The silky texture on the tongue, makes a wine-derived alcohol spirit a pleasure to sip straight up.

If you have spent any time at all in your local liquor store you have noticed the proliferation of flavored Vodka courtesy of the big commercial distillers. The consumer is slowly catching on that these Vodkas are all chemically flavored with harsh aldehyde type chemicals. Sadly, many of these chemical flavors already legally appear in our food system which is why the large distillers have so easily been able to populate liquor store shelves with flavored Vodka ranging from whipped cream flavor to bubble gum flavor. With the consumer starting to lean more intently towards real food, can a shift towards *real* flavored spirits be far behind? In my opinion, the days of chemically flavored Vodka are numbered. There is a huge opportunity for the craft distiller who wants to flavor Vodkas with all natural fruit syrups or even with real fruit. One craft distiller that is having good success at natural flavoring is Legend Distilling in Naramata, British Columbia. Their Honey/Rhubarb Vodka released for the 2015 season was excellent. The big hit in 2016 so far seems to be their Naramata Sour Cherry Vodka. Another craft distiller having good luck with natural flavor is Big Rig Distilling in Nisku, Alberta. I am told their Blueberry Vodka is a big seller. It need not be fruit juices that provide the flavor. Urban Distilleries in Kelowna, British Columbia makes a Dill Vodka, a Peri Peri Chile Vodka and a Vanilla Bean Vodka and all are strong sellers.

Whisky: the definition of a Whisky is an alcoholic distillate or mix of such distillates made from cereal grain. A Whisky by definition may contain caramel and flavoring. Notice that this definition contains no reference to barrel aging. A craft distiller could then make a distillate from a grain or grains of his or her choice and sell it un-aged to the consumer at a suitable alcoholic strength.

This definition is driving the white Whisky market. One product that appears in most liquor stores is *White Owl Whisky* from Highwood Distillers in High River, Alberta. In my workshops, I have yet to find anyone who adamantly enjoys this product on its own. Similarly, Dillons has its *White Rye* product made from 100% Rye grain. Workshop participants note the pleasant spiciness of the Rye grain in this well-made product, but comment that they probably would not buy it as a sipping Whisky. A new product that is now available is *Virgin Spirits* from Dub'h Glas Distilling in Oliver, British Columbia. Thanks to a special strain of yeast and a carefully controlled fermentation temperature, this white Whisky delivers pleasant fruity notes on the nose and on the palate. It will be interesting to see if the consumer starts questing after this product in large numbers.

In my workshops I often do a small experiment that is well received.

I add few Blackberries or Raspberries to a measured quantity of a white Whisky and let the berries soak for 3 days. The result is a pleasant tasting spirit that a consumer could sip straight up or possibly mix with a slight splash of soda water.

The bottom line is - there are some serious opportunities awaiting the craft distiller who can take a white Whisky and infuse it with fruit or natural fruit syrup. Keep it real, keep it genuine and the consumer will notice.

Malt Whisky: take the above definition of Whisky and alter it slightly to read that *malted* grain must be used and you are well on your way to understanding what a Malt Whisky is. The definition tightens up matters a bit more with the requirement that a Malt Whisky must have the taste and character generally attributed to a Malt Whisky.

One of the pioneers in the Malt Whisky arena in Canada has been Glen Breton Distilling from Nova Scotia. Glen Breton has aged their product offerings for up to 15 years in some cases.

But, notice that this definition, just like the definition for Whisky, contains no age requirement. As a craft distiller, you can use malted grains to make a distillate and then very creatively expose this distillate to oak chips to infuse some oaky notes into the product. Urban Distilleries of Kelowna, BC exposes its distillate (made from 80 % malted wheat/20 % malted barley) to medium toasted French oak chips for a proprietary period of time to infuse an oak tenor into the spirit. At bottling time, each bottle further receives a small piece of oak French Oak stave to provide for more layers of flavor development as the bottles sit on the customer's liquor cabinet shelf. On the palate, this product delivers a delicious, almost buttery texture. Sperling Distillery in Regina, Saskatchewan exposes its distillate (made from 100 % malted rye) to French Oak chips for a period of time. On the palate, this Special Rye is truly wonderful.

Similarly, a craft distiller could place some Malt Whisky distillate in oak barrels for any length of time to infuse an oak tenor into the spirit. The barrels could be new or they could be used. They could be North American oak or European oak. Think creatively. Think outside the box. The consumer will notice.

Canadian Whisky, Canadian Rye Whisky, Rye Whisky: produce a Whisky or a Malt Whisky as per the above stated definitions. Barrel age that Whisky or Malt Whisky in *small wood* (a wood container less than 700 liters in volume) for a minimum of three years. This will allow you to call the resulting product a Canadian Whisky, a Canadian Rye Whisky or a Rye Whisky.

The definition further stipulates that the product must be mashed, distilled and aged in Canada. The bottling strength must not be less than 40 % alcohol by volume. Caramel coloring may be added as can flavor preparations. As far as the aging period is concerned, three years is the minimum, so a distiller could age it for longer.

The definition states that no person shall make any statement concerning the age of a Canadian Whisky other than for the period during which the Whisky has been held in small wood. Personally, I find these definitions very loosely worded. Loose word structures are what clever lawyers can take advantage of. Take the case of a product made by Highwood Distillers in High River, Alberta called *Century 21 Reserve*. At first glance, this would appear to be a 21 year old Canadian Whisky. But when one looks at the price tag, some suspicion enters the mind. The price tag at around $50 per bottle is too low for something that is 21 years old. Next time you are at your local liquor store, check the prices for 21 year old Scotches and you will see what I mean. What likely happened in this case is the company did have some 21 year old product in inventory. To produce *Century 21 Reserve*,

I rather suspect this older Whisky was blended with a much younger, cheaper distillate. The attendant color was then tweaked by the addition of some caramel coloring. So, there are no lies here. There is 21 year old product in the bottle, just not all the product is 21 years old.

Such are the subtle legal nuances of how Canadian Whisky can be altered. Take your pick of which name you want to apply to a Whisky, Canadian Whisky, Canadian Rye Whisky or Rye Whisky. Nowhere in the verbiage does it stipulate how much Rye grain must be contained in the mash. A distiller following this definition could make a distillate from Wheat and blend it with the tiniest amount of Rye grain distillate and call it a Canadian Rye Whisky. Such seems to be the case with *Highwood Distillers Canadian Rye Whisky* which is made from primarily Wheat.

Many Canadian Whiskies are largely formulated from Corn based distillate – a fact that few consumers are aware of. This Corn based distillate is then flavored with Rye based distillate to deliver the desired taste profile. As a craft distiller, do not be afraid to use Corn in your recipe formulations. You will likely find your product well received by the consumer's palate. After all, that palate has been unknowingly sipping Corn based distillate for decades now.

There is one Canadian Whisky that deserves a very special bit of recognition for its departure from the norm. Alberta Premium Canadian Rye Whisky is a stellar example of what a Canadian Rye Whisky should be. It is in fact made from 100 % Rye grain. A delicious product without doubt, with a taste profile that craft distillers should aspire to.

Flavored Whisky: some time ago, the large commercial distillers approached the government regulators seeking a way to shave time off the three year aging regimen. The concession that was granted stated that a Canadian Whisky can be given a flavoring preparation and then aged for only two years. Now you know why Crown Royal Maple Whisky and Crown Royal Apple Whisky were created. One year less of aging means cash flow one year sooner.

Rum: in Canada the definition for Rum states that Rum must be made from sugar cane or sugar cane products. Sugar cane products are generally accepted to mean molasses. Molasses is the remaining sludge from the sugar extraction process.

The question has often been posed to me - what about table sugar which is technically a sugar cane product? My answer is that sugar in and of itself will produce a distillate that is very clean in taste profile and thus lacking in the traditional Rum flavor that consumers associate with Rum.

The Rum definition goes on to state that Rum must be aged for one year minimum in *small wood.* If aging in wood is required, and if wood aging imparts some coloration to the distillate, how then do the large distillers make White Rum? The answer is filtration. By passing the aged product through filter media, any barrel-derived color can be removed. The definition further states that caramel, botanicals or flavoring preparation may be added. Now you know where Captain Morgan Spiced Rum comes from. It is simply Rum distillate to which has been added some flavoring preparation to impart the spiced profile.

Another question that arises is what if one could obtain molasses from the Roger's Sugar factory in Taber, Alberta? In fact it is easy to obtain such molasses. Visit your local animal feed supply store and ask for a pail of feed molasses. It will have a soupier consistency than the molasses you see at the grocery store. But it works very well for home distilling making Rum and I have plenty of personal experience to support this assertion. The sugar factory in Taber, Alberta extracts sugar from sugar beets (and not sugar cane). The use of their molasses will place you at odds with the Rum definition. A sugar beet is far different from a sugar cane. A Rum made from sugar beet molasses would have to be called a Rum Flavored Spirit Beverage or something similar in order to remain compliant with the crc 870 definitions. One craft distiller that is using this molasses from Taber, Alberta is Big Rig Distilling in Nisku, Alberta. Their product is called *Brum*, which is a clever play on the words beet and rum. To their distillate they add some flavoring preparation to produce a sweet tasting product that has been quite well received in Workshops. In your travels, if you are looking for an example of a very good craft distilled Rum made from sugar cane molasses, try to find some rum from Ironworks Distillery in Lunenburg, Nova Scotia. This Rum is regularly sipped in our Workshops to great acclaim. One other that I have recently stumbled upon is Leatherback Rum from North of 7 Distilling in Ottawa, Ontario. This distillate has been made from 100 % molasses. The dark color and slight smoky notes derived from barrel aging make this Rum a divine inspiration indeed. I have now added this product to my tasting lineup in my Workshops.

Gin: in Canada, the definition of a Gin states that one must start with alcohol from food sources. This means alcohol distilled from grains, potatoes, grapes or fruit. Take your pick.

To that alcohol, one will add juniper berries and then re-distill the alcohol. Heavy emphasis here on the word re-distill. There are jurisdictions in the world that simply allow botanicals to be soaked in alcohol to create a Gin. In Canada, we must re-distill the alcohol in which we have soaked the botanicals.

If you are thinking that Gin contains more than just juniper, you are correct. The definition allows for the addition of other botanicals, a sweetening agent and even flavoring preparations to maintain a uniform flavor profile. I have seen craft distillers add up to a dozen different botanicals to their Gins. If no sweetening agent has been added, the Gin maker has the privilege of calling the product London Dry Gin. Most craft distillers that I have seen are simply calling their product Gin. London Dry Gin seems to be something best suited for those classic Gins from the U.K. including Gordon's, Bombay Sapphire and Tanqueray.

One may also start seeing the expression New Western Dry Gin. I have raised this issue with the Canadian Food Inspection Agency and they advise that this expression, although not codified into crc 870, simply refers to a Gin that has less emphasis on juniper and more emphasis on other botanicals. I have seen only a small handful of craft distillers adopt this moniker. The vast majority are simply calling their product Gin.

The next evolution in Gin that I am seeing evidence of is barrel rested Gin. Craft distillers are obtaining ex-sherry casks, ex-port casks and ex-cognac casks. They are resting their Gins in these casks for up to six months and then bottling. Some of the end results I have tasted are truly exceptional. One that stands out is from Black Fox Distilling in Saskatoon, Saskatchewan. They rest their Gin in a new charred oak barrel for 6 months before bottling it. The notes of oak and vanilla on the palate blend harmoniously with the notes from Juniper and the other botanicals.

I prefer to think of Gin as a blank artistic canvas. As a craft distiller, you can get out your paint brush and create your masterpiece. My experiences have shown that lavender can impart a delicious taste profile to Gin. Perhaps the best Gin I have had anywhere is *Spirit Bear Gin* from Urban Distilleries in Kelowna, British Columbia. The gentle use of lavender in this Gin makes for an absolutely superb sipping product. As an extension of the standard 5-day Workshops, I have now started offering 1-day Gin Master Classes in which participants devise recipes and then get to distill those recipes on a small Alembic still. We are discovering that additives such as apple, grapefruit and even parsnip can add unique twists to the taste of a Gin. The sky is the limit. As a craft distiller, think outside the box. Think creatively.

Canadian Brandy: in Canada, if one obtains grapes and ferments them in Canada and subsequently distills the resulting wine, the distillate can be termed a Canadian Brandy. Notice in this definition there is no requirement as to where the grapes must come from. Brandy is not a big seller, probably because the handful of distillers that make the stuff have never aggressively marketed the product. The definition goes on to say that one can add fruit, botanicals and flavor preparations to Brandy.

My small scale research has demonstrated that Brandy can be given a unique twist by macerating grapefruit peel and orange peel in it and then adding a touch of honey for a bit of sweetness. I have had similar successes with the maceration of mandarin orange pieces in the brandy.

As a craft distiller - think outside the box and come at the consumer with a brandy they have never seen before and you might be surprised at what happens.

Dried Fruit Brandy: take the above definition for Brandy and adjust it so that a distillate is produced from a fermented mash of dried fruit and you have the basis for a Dried Fruit Brandy.

Fruit Brandy: take fruit wine or a mixture of such wines and distill. Alternatively, take a mash of sound, ripe fruits (other than grapes) or a mixture of such fruits. Ferment the mash and then distill. The resulting products can be called Fruit Brandy. Caramel color, botanicals and flavoring preparations may be added under this definition.

Grappa: when a wine maker presses grapes, the remaining mass of skins and seeds is termed *pomace*. Take that pomace, rehydrate with water and add yeast to ferment whatever remaining bits of fermentable sugars are in the pomace and then distill the resulting product and you will have a distillate that you can call Grappa.

There is one hitch, however. The name Grappa is trade protected by Italy. In Canada, you will have to add one additional descriptor to your Grappa. Call it Okanagan Grappa, Gewurztraminer Grappa, Muscat Grappa or some such name and you will be in compliance with the trade protected name. Typically not a big seller in Canada, Grappa is something that a craft distiller might want to offer seasonally in limited quantities.

Liqueur: take alcohol from food sources and mix it, infuse it or macerate it with fruits, flowers, leaves or botancals. Alternatively, take alcohol from food sources and re-distill it with fruits, flowers, leaves or botancals. The resulting product will be well on its way to being called a Liqueur. To complete the process, add a minimum of 2.5 % sweetener and ensure that the end product contains not less than 23 % alcohol by volume. Most Liqueurs on liquor store shelves will be in the 25 to 30 % alcohol by volume range. One efficient way of producing a Liqueur is to take alcohol, mix it with fruit syrup concentrates and liquid invert sugar. Two outstanding examples of such are Urban Distilleries *Raspberry Liqueur* and *Blackberry Liqueur*. Another product that has just hit the market is *Manitou* from Legend Distilling in Naramata, British Columbia. This product has been made by steeping orange peels and sumac berries in alcohol for a proprietary period of time. Some sweetener is then added and the product proofed to 30 % alcohol/volume. I routinely serve this product in Workshops to great acclaim.

Vermouth: Take alcohol from food sources, add botanicals, aromatics or flavoring preparations. Add white wine and ensure that the alcoholic strength is no higher than 20 %. This is the definition of a Vermouth. When the consumer sees Vermouth, he or she will instinctively think of the commercial stuff that one adds to martinis. For an example of a brilliantly crafted Vermouth, Odd Society Spirits in Vancouver, British Columbia makes a Vermouth that quite frankly makes my knees weak – it is just that good. I enjoy a splash of their Vermouth over ice. I could sip this libation all day long.

Restrictions: There are many product names that we cannot use in Canada. As noted above, naming a spirit just as *Grappa* is in violation of trade agreements with Italy. *Grappa di Ticino* is a name protected by Switzerland. The names *Jagertee* and *Jagatee* are protected by Austria. Spirits named *Korn* and *Kornbrand* are protected by the Germans and Austrians. The name *Ouzo* is protected by Greece. *Pacharan* is a name protected by Spain. *Scotch* and *Scotch Whisky* are the sole domain of Scotland. *Irish Whisky* is likewise sole domain of Ireland. Brandies by the names *Armagnac* and *Cognac* are the property of France only. *Bourbon* and *Bourbon Whisky* are names closely protected by the United States. Similarly, *Tennessee Whisky* is the domain of the State of Tennessee. *Tequila* is to be made in Mexico and even then only in a certain part of Mexico. *Mezcal* is also protected by the Mexicans.

Caribbean Rum can only be sold under that name if it is fermented and distilled from cane sugar in a Commonwealth Caribbean country. A Canadian distiller can import Rum in bulk quantity from a Commonwealth Caribbean nation for the purposes of blending it with other Caribbean Rum and then sell it under the name Caribbean Rum. Likewise, a Canadian distiller can import Rum in bulk quantity from a Commonwealth Caribbean nation and blend it with up to 1.5 % Canadian Rum by volume and sell it as Caribbean Rum. A Canadian distiller can import Rum in bulk quantity from a Commonwealth Caribbean nation and blend it with distilled or purified water to proof it down to a more suitable alcoholic strength. Lastly, a Canadian distiller can import Rum in bulk quantity from a

Commonwealth Caribbean nation and blend it with caramel to alter the color profile. The Caribbean Commonwealth nations are Anguilla, Antigua, Barbados, Bahamas, Belize, Bermuda, British Virgin Islands, Cayman Islands, Dominica, Grenada, Guyana, Jamaica, Montserrat, St. Kitts and Nevis, Saint Lucia, St. Vincent and the Grenadines, Trinidad and Tobago, and Turks and Caicos.

REFERENCES

A History of Vodka, W. Pokhlebkin, 1991, Verso Publishing, UK.

http://laws-lois.justice.gc.ca/eng/regulations/C.R.C.,_c._870/page-55.html#docCont.

If this link does not work properly, do an online search using the term 'crc 870 spirits definitions'

AMERICA

The following is a discussion of the definitions as laid down by the United States Alcohol and Tobacco Tax and Trade Bureau (TTB).

Grain Spirit/Neutral Spirit: in America, a craft distiller can make Neutral Spirits or Grain Spirits. Grain Spirits are made from a mash of cereal grains and distilled to 95 % alcohol or above (190 proof). Neutral Spirits are made from any material (ie. grains, surplus wine, fruit) and distilled to 95 % alcohol or above (190 proof). If bottled, these spirits must have a minimum of 40 % alcohol (80 proof).

Vodka: in America, Vodka is defined as Grain Spirit or Neutral Spirit treated with charcoal or other materials so as to be without distinctive character, aroma, taste or color. These definitions underscore the importance of being aware of subtle differences in definitions from country to country. In America, drinks giant Diageo has a Vodka brand called Ciroc which has been distilled from surplus wine. This same product in Canada cannot be called a Vodka because the Canadian definitions require Vodka to be made from cereal grains. Ciroc in Canada will be found in the Vodka section of liquor stores, but it will be labelled as a Spirit Drink.

Whisky: in America, a Whisky is defined as an alcoholic spirit distilled from a fermented mash of grain at less than 95 % alcohol by volume (190 proof) having the taste, aroma and characteristics generally attributed to Whisky and bottled at not less than 40 % alcohol by volume (80 proof). Under this umbrella definition are several sub-categories.

> **Bourbon Whisky:** Whisky produced in the U.S. at not exceeding 80 % alcohol by volume (160 proof) from a fermented mash of not less than 51 % Corn and stored at not more than 62.5 % alcohol by volume (125 proof) in charred new oak containers.
>
> **Rye Whisky:** in the Bourbon definition, replace the word Corn with the word Rye.
>
> **Wheat Whisky:** in the Bourbon definition, replace the word Rye with the word Wheat.
>
> **Malt Whisky:** in the Bourbon definition, replace the word Wheat with the expression malted Barley.

Rye Malt Whisky: in the Bourbon definition, replace malted Barley with the expression malted Rye.

Corn Whisky: is similar to the definition of Bourbon, except that a Corn Whisky must not be exposed to aging in a charred wood container. New oak and used oak containers can be used so long as they have not been charred.

Straight Whiskies: in the TTB definitions, special treatment is accorded to whiskies that have been aged for a minimum prescribed time.

Straight Bourbon Whisky: a Bourbon Whisky as per the above definitions that has been aged for two or more years.

Straight Rye Whisky: a Rye Whisky aged for two or more years

Straight Wheat Whisky: a Wheat Whisky aged for two or more years.

Straight Malt Whisky: a Malt Whisky aged for two or more years.

Straight Rye Malt Whisky: a Rye Malt Whisky aged for two or more years.

Straight Corn Whisky: a Corn Whisky as per the above definition aged for two or more years.

Straight Whisky: TTB definitions allow for something called a Straight Whisky which is a Whisky containing not more than 51 % of any one type of grain.

For the above listed products (except Corn products) an age statement is required if the aging period has been less than 4 years. Aging periods greater than four years do not require a statement on the label, but some distillers choose to add an age statement regardless.

For the above listed products (except Corn products) the statement **"Bottled in Bond"** shall reflect a product aged a minimum of four years, made by a single distiller in a single season and bottled at 50 % alcohol (100 proof).

Blended Whisky: a minimum of 20 % by volume Straight Whisky mixed with any other Whisky or with Grain Spirit/Neutral Spirit.

Blended Bourbon Whisky: a blend containing not less than 51 % Straight Bourbon Whisky.

Blended Rye Whisky: a blend containing not less than 51 % Straight Rye Whisky.

Blended Wheat Whisky: a blend containing not less than 51 % Straight Wheat Whisky.

Blended Malt Whisky: a blend containing not less than 51 % Straight Malt Whisky.

Blended Rye Malt Whisky: a blend containing not less than 51 % Straight Malt Whisky.

Blended Corn Whisky: a blend containing not less than 51 % Straight Corn Whisky.

For the above listed blended products (except the blended Corn

Whisky), age statements must reflect the youngest component of the blend.

Gin: in America, Gin is defined as an alcoholic spirit with a main characteristic flavor derived from juniper berries produced by distillation or mixing of spirits with juniper berries and other aromatics or extracts derived from these materials and bottled at not less than 40 % alcohol by volume (80 proof).

Under this umbrella definition are some sub-categories.

> **Distilled Gin:** is a spirit made by distilling a mash with or over juniper berries and other aromatics or their extracts, essences or flavors.

> **Re-distilled Gin:** a spirit made by the Gin produced by re-distillation of distilled spirits with or over juniper berries and other aromatics or their extracts, essences or flavors.

> **Compounded Gin:** a Gin produced by mixing Neutral Spirits with juniper berries and other aromatics or their extracts, essences or flavors.

Brandy: in America, a Brandy is defined as a spirit distilled from the fermented juice, mash or wine of fruit or from its residue at less than 95 % alcohol by volume (190 proof) having the taste, aroma and characteristics generally attributed to brandy and bottled at not less than 40% alcohol by volume (80 proof). Under this definition are some sub-categories.

> **Fruit Brandy:** Brandy distilled solely from the fermented juice or mash of whole, sound, ripe fruit or from standard fruit wine, with or without the addition of not more than 20

% by weight of the pomace of such juice or wine or 30 % by volume of the lees of such wine or both.

AppleJack: is a Brandy made from apples.

Kirchwasser: is a Brandy made from cherries.

Slivovitz: is a Brandy made from plums.

Dried Fruit Brandy: is a Brandy distilled from sound, dried fruit. The name of the product must contain the name of the fruit (ie. Dried Apricot Brandy)

Pomace or Marc Brandy: is a Brandy distilled from the skin and pulp of sound, ripe grapes after the withdrawal of the juice. If fruit other than grapes is used, the name of that fruit must be reflected in the name of the product (ie. Apple Pomace Brandy).

Rum: in America, a rum is a spirit distilled from the fermented juice of sugar cane, sugar cane syrup, sugar cane molasses or other sugar cane by-products at less than 95 % alcohol by volume (190 proof) having the taste, aroma and characteristics generally attributed to rum and bottled at not less than 40 % alcohol by volume (80 proof).

Liqueur: in America, a Liqueur is a flavored spirit product containing not less than 2½ % by weight sugar, dextrose, levulose or a combination thereof made by mixing or redistilling any class or type of spirits with or over fruits, flowers, plants or pure juices therefrom or other natural flavoring materials or with extracts derived from infusions, percolation or maceration of such materials. Under this umbrella definition, there are a few noteworthy sub-categories.

Rye Liqueur: a Liqueur made with not less than 51 % Rye Whisky, Straight Rye Whisky or Whisky distilled from Rye mash bottled at not less than 30 % alcohol by volume (60 proof).

Bourbon Liqueur: a Liqueur produced in the U.S. with the predominant characteristic flavor of Bourbon Whiskey made with not less than 51 % Bourbon Whisky, Straight Bourbon Whisky or Whisky distilled from Bourbon mash bottled at not less than 30 % alcohol by volume (60 proof).

Gin Liqueur: a Liqueur with the predominant characteristic flavor of Gin made with Gin as the exclusive distilled spirits base, bottled at not less than 30 % alcohol by volume (60 proof).

Brandy Liqueur: a Liqueur with the predominant characteristic flavor of Brandy made with Brandy as the exclusive distilled spirits base, bottled at not less than 30 % alcohol by volume (60 proof).

REFERENCES

http://www.ttb.gov/spirits/bam/chapter4.pdf

http://www.ttb.gov/spirits/bam/chapter8.pdf

EUROPEAN UNION

The following is a brief look at the very restrictive spirits definitions as laid down by the European Parliament. These definitions will apply to a craft distiller seeking to operate in the United Kingdom. Regulation (EC) No 110/2008 contains the definition, description, presentation, labelling and the protection of geographical indications of spirit drinks.

The ethyl alcohol used in the production of spirit drinks and all of their components shall not be of any origin other than agricultural, within the meaning of Annex I to the Treaty.

Ethyl alcohol of agricultural origin: ethyl alcohol of agricultural origin possesses the following properties:

(a) organoleptic characteristics: no detectable taste other than that of the raw material;

(b) minimum alcoholic strength by volume: 96.0 %;

(c) maximum level of residues:

(i) total acidity, expressed in grams of acetic acid per hectolitre of 100 % vol. alcohol: 1.5,

(ii) esters expressed in grams of ethyl acetate per hectolitre of 100 % vol. alcohol: 1.3,

(iii) aldehydes expressed in grams of acetaldehyde per hectolitre of 100 % vol. alcohol: 0.5,

(iv) higher alcohols expressed in grams of methyl2 propanol1 per hectolitre of 100 % vol. alcohol: 0.5,

(v) methanol expressed in grams per hectolitre of 100 % vol. alcohol: 30,

(vi) dry extract expressed in grams per hectolitre of 100 % vol. alcohol: 1.5,

(vii) volatile bases containing nitrogen expressed in grams of nitrogen per hectolitre of 100 % vol. alcohol: 0.1,

(viii) furfural: not detectable.

This tight definition explains why so many Gin craft distillers starting up in the U.K. are purchasing neutral grain alcohol rather than making their own alcohol. I have heard stories of craft distillers being severely chastised for failing to abide by this definition when authorities investigated the craft distillers at the behest of one of the big commercial distillers seeking to interrupt the craft distilling movement.

Sweetening: sweetening means using one or more of the following products in the preparation of spirit drinks:

(a) semi-white sugar, white sugar, extra-white sugar, dextrose, fructose, glucose syrup, sugar solution, invert sugar solution, invert sugar syrup, as defined in Council Directive 2001/111/EC of 20 December 2001 relating to certain sugars intended for human consumption;
(b) rectified concentrated grape must, concentrated grape must, fresh grape must;
(c) burned sugar, which is the product obtained exclusively from the controlled heating of sucrose without bases, mineral acids or other chemical additives;
(d) honey as defined in Council Directive 2001/110/EC of 20 December 2001 relating to honey;
(e) carob syrup;
(f) any other natural carbohydrate substances having a similar effect to those products.

Rum: in the E.U., Rum is a spirit drink produced exclusively by alcoholic fermentation and distillation, either from molasses or syrup produced in the manufacture of cane sugar or from sugar-cane juice itself and distilled at less than 96 % vol. so that the distillate has the discernible specific organoleptic characteristics of Rum, or a spirit drink produced exclusively by alcoholic fermentation and distillation of sugar-cane juice which has the aromatic characteristics specific to Rum and a volatile substances content equal to or exceeding 225 grams per hectoliter of 100 % vol. alcohol.

Rum shall not be flavored and the minimum alcoholic strength of Rum shall be 37.5 %. Only caramel color may be added to Rum to adjust color.

Whisky: in the E.U., a Whisky takes on a definition similar to that of Canada. Whisky is an alcoholic distillate made from a mash of grain. It shall be subject to one or more distillations so that so that the distillate has an aroma and taste derived from the raw materials used. The final distillate shall be aged in wooden casks not exceeding 700 liters in size for three years. The minimum alcoholic strength shall be 40 %. Whisky shall not be sweetened or flavored. Only caramel may be added for color adjustment.

Grain Spirit: in the E.U., a Grain Spirit is an alcoholic distillate made from a mash of cereal grains and having organoleptic characteristics derived from the raw materials used. The minimum alcoholic strength shall be 35 %. The distillate may not be flavored. Only caramel may be added for color adjustment.

Wine Spirit: in the E.U., Wine Spirit can be produced exclusively by the distillation at less than 86 % vol. of wine. The volatile substances in a wine spirit shall be equal to or exceeding 125 grams per hectolitre of 100 % vol. alcohol. The maximum methanol content of 200 grams per hectolitre of 100 % vol. alcohol. The minimum alcoholic strength of a wine spirit shall be 37.5 %. No flavoring may be added except caramel for color adjustment.

Brandy: in the E.U., Brandy shall be produced from Wine Spirit, distilled at less than 94.8 % vol., provided that that distillate does not exceed a maximum of 50 % of the alcoholic content of the finished product. Brandy shall be matured for at least one year in oak receptacles or for at least six months in oak casks with a capacity of less than 1,000 litres. The minimum alcoholic strength shall be 36 %. The volatile substances in a wine spirit shall be equal to or exceeding 125 grams per hectolitre of 100 % vol. alcohol. The maximum methanol content of 200 grams per hectolitre of 100 % vol. alcohol. No flavoring may be added except caramel for color adjustment.

Grape Marc Spirit: in the E.U., Grape Marc Spirit is produced exclusively from grape marc fermented and distilled either directly by water vapor or after water has been added. A quantity of lees may be added to the grape marc that does not exceed 25 kg of lees per 100 kg of grape marc used. The quantity of alcohol derived from the lees shall not exceed 35 % of the total quantity of alcohol in the finished product. The distillation shall be carried out in the presence of the marc itself at less than 86 % vol. alcohol. Re-distillation at the same alcoholic strength is authorized. Marc contains a quantity of volatile substances equal to or exceeding 140 grams per hectolitre of 100 % vol. alcohol and has a maximum methanol content of 1,000 grams per hectolitre of 100 % vol. alcohol.

The minimum alcoholic strength by volume of grape marc spirit or grape marc shall be 37.5 %. No addition of alcohol as defined in Annex I(5), diluted or not, shall take place. Grape marc spirit or grape marc shall not be flavored. This shall not exclude traditional production methods. Grape marc spirit or grape marc may only contain added caramel as a means to adapt color.

Fruit Marc Spirit: in the E.U., a Fruit Marc Spirit is obtained exclusively by fermentation and distillation at less than 86 % vol. of fruit marc except grape marc contains a minimum quantity of volatile substances of 200 grams per hectolitre of 100 % vol. alcohol; the maximum methanol content shall be 1,500 grams per hectolitre of

100 % vol. alcohol; the maximum hydrocyanic acid content shall be 7 grams per hectolitre of 100 % vol. alcohol in the case of stone-fruit marc spirit.

The minimum alcoholic strength shall be 37.5%. No flavoring shall be added. Caramel can be added to adjust color.

Fruit spirit: in the E.U., a Fruit Spirit is a spirit drink produced exclusively by the alcoholic fermentation and distillation of fleshy fruit or must of such fruit, berries or vegetables, with or without stones, distilled at less than 86 % vol. so that the distillate has an aroma and taste derived from the raw materials distilled, having a quantity of volatile substances equal to or exceeding 200 grams per hectolitre of 100 % vol. alcohol, in the case of stone-fruit spirits, having a hydrocyanic acid content not exceeding 7 grams per hectolitre of 100 % vol. alcohol.

The maximum methanol content of Fruit Spirit shall be 1,000 grams per hectolitre of 100 % vol. alcohol. However for the following fruit spirits the maximum methanol content shall be:

(i) 1,200 grams per hectolitre of 100 % vol. alcohol obtained from the following fruits or berries: plum, quetsch, apple, pear, raspberries, blackberries, apricots, peaches.

ii) 1,350 grams per hectolitre of 100 % vol. alcohol obtained from the following fruits or berries: Williams pears, redcurrants, blackcurrants, rowanberries, elderberries, quinces, juniper berries.

The minimum alcoholic strength by volume of fruit spirit shall be 37.5 %. No addition of alcohol as defined in Annex I(5), diluted or not, shall take place. Fruit spirit shall not be flavored.

Vodka: in the E.U., Vodka is a spirit drink produced from ethyl alcohol of agricultural origin obtained following fermentation with yeast from either:

(i) potatoes and/or cereals, or

(ii) other agricultural raw materials, distilled and/or rectified so that the organoleptic characteristics of the raw materials used and by-products formed in fermentation are selectively reduced.

This process may be followed by re-distillation and/or treatment with appropriate processing aids, including treatment with activated charcoal, to give it special organoleptic characteristics. Maximum levels of residue for ethyl alcohol of agricultural origin shall meet those laid down in Annex I, except that the methanol content shall not exceed 10 grams per hectolitre of 100 % vol. alcohol.

Flavored Vodka: flavored Vodka is Vodka which has been given a predominant flavor other than that of the raw materials. The minimum alcoholic strength by volume of flavored Vodka shall be 37.5%. Flavored Vodka may be sweetened, blended, flavored, matured or colored. Flavored Vodka may also be sold under the name of any predominant flavor with the word 'Vodka'.

Gin: in the E.U., Gin, is a juniper-flavored spirit drink produced by flavoring organoleptically suitable Ethyl alcohol of agricultural origin with juniper berries (Juniperus communis L.). The minimum alcoholic strength by volume of Gin shall be 37.5 %. Only natural and/or nature-identical flavoring substances as defined in Article 1(2)(b)(i) and (ii) of Directive 88/388/EEC and/or flavoring preparations as defined in Article 1(2)(c) of that Directive shall be used for the production of Gin so that the taste is predominantly that of juniper.

Distilled Gin: Distilled Gin is a juniper-flavored spirit drink produced exclusively by re-distilling organoleptically suitable ethyl alcohol of agricultural origin of an appropriate quality with an initial alcoholic strength of at least 96 % vol. in stills traditionally used for Gin, in the presence of juniper berries (Juniperus communis L.) and of other natural botanicals provided that the juniper taste is predominant.

The minimum alcoholic strength by volume of distilled Gin shall be 37.5 %.

London Gin: London Gin is a type of distilled gin obtained exclusively from ethyl alcohol of agricultural origin, with a maximum methanol content of 5 grams per hectolitre of 100 % vol. alcohol, whose flavor is introduced exclusively through the re-distillation in traditional stills of ethyl alcohol in the presence of all the natural plant materials used. The resultant distillate shall contain at least 70 % alcohol by volume. Where any further ethyl alcohol of agricultural origin is added it must be consistent with the characteristics listed in Annex I(1), but with a maximum methanol content of 5 grams per hectolitre of 100 % vol. alcohol. London Gin must not contain added sweetening exceeding 0.1 gram of sugars per litre of the final product. No colorants are allowed. London Gin shall not contain any other added ingredients other than water.

The minimum alcoholic strength by volume of London Gin shall be 37.5 %.The term London Gin may be supplemented by the term 'dry'.

Liqueur: Liqueur is a spirit drink having a minimum sugar content, expressed as invert sugar, of:

— 70 grams per litre for cherry liqueurs the ethyl alcohol of which consists exclusively of cherry spirit,

— 80 grams per litre for gentian or similar liqueurs prepared with gentian or similar plants as the sole aromatic substance,

— 100 grams per litre in all other cases;

Liqueur can be produced by flavoring ethyl alcohol of agricultural origin or a distillate of agricultural origin or one or more spirit drinks or a mixture thereof, sweetened and with the addition of products of agricultural origin or foodstuffs such as cream, milk or other milk products, fruit, wine or aromatised wine as defined in Council Regulation (EEC) No 1601/91 of 10 June 1991.

The minimum alcoholic strength by volume of Liqueur shall be 15%. Only natural flavoring substances and preparations as defined in Article 1(2)(b)(i) and Article 1(2)(c) of Directive 88/388/EEC and nature-identical flavoring substances and preparations as defined in Article 1(2)(b)(ii) of that Directive may be used in the preparation of Liqueur.

Nature-identical flavoring substances and preparations as defined in Article 1(2)(b)(ii) of that Directive shall not be used in the preparation of the following Liqueurs:

(i) Fruit liqueurs:

blackcurrant, cherry, raspberry, mulberry, bilberry, citrus fruit, cloudberry, arctic bramble, cranberry, lingonberry, sea buckthorn, pineapple;

(ii) plant liqueurs:

— mint, gentian, aniseed, génépi, vulnerary.

(d) The following compound terms may be used in the presentation of Liqueurs produced in the Community where Ethyl alcohol of agricultural origin is used to mirror established production methods:

— prune brandy, orange brandy, apricot brandy, cherry brandy, solbaerrom, (also called blackcurrant rum).

As regards the labelling and presentation of those Liqueurs, the compound term must appear on the labelling in one line in uniform characters of the same font and color and the word 'Liqueur' must appear in immediate proximity in characters no smaller than that font. If the alcohol does not come from the spirit drink indicated, its origin must be shown on the labelling in the same visual field as the compound term and the word 'Liqueur' either by stating the type of agricultural alcohol or by the words 'agricultural alcohol' preceded on each occasion by 'made from' or 'made using'.

Sloe Gin: Sloe Gin is a Liqueur produced by maceration of sloes in Gin with the possible addition of sloe juice. The minimum alcoholic strength by volume of Sloe Gin shall be 25 %. Only natural flavoring substances and preparations as defined in Article 1(2)(b)(i) and Article 1(2)(c) of Directive 88/388/EEC may be used in the preparation of Sloe Gin. The sales denomination may be supplemented by the term 'Liqueur'.

Scotch Whisky: The European Union has permitted the UK to introduce a specific definition covering Scotch Whisky.

Scotch Whisky means Whisky (distilled and matured in Scotland) as conforming to the - The Scotch Whisky Act 1988.

For the purpose of the Scotch Whisky Act 1988 "Scotch Whisky" means Whisky –

(a) which has been produced at a distillery in Scotland from water and malted barley (to which only whole grains of other cereals may be added) all of which have been -

(i) processed at that distillery into a mash;

(ii) converted into a fermentable substrate only by endogenous enzyme systems; and

(iii) fermented only by the action of yeast;

(b) which has been distilled at an alcoholic strength by volume of less than 94.8 per cent so that the distillate has an aroma and taste derived from raw materials used in, and the method of, its production;

(c) which has been matured in an excise warehouse in Scotland in oak casks of a capacity not exceeding 700 liters, the period of that maturation being not less than 3 years;

(d) which retains the color, aroma and taste derived from the raw materials used in the method of its production and maturation; and

(e) to which no other substance other than water and spirit caramel has been added-The Scotch Whisky Order 1990.

Irish Whisky: The European Union has permitted a definition for Irish Whisky as per the Irish Whisky Act of 1980. There are three varieties of Irish Whisky:

"Pot Still Irish Whiskey/Irish Pot Still Whiskey" is defined as a spirit distilled from a mash of a combination of malted barley, unmalted barley and other unmalted cereals. The mash must contain a minimum of 30 % malted barley and a minimum of 30% unmalted barley and be:

a) saccharified by the diastase of malt contained therein, with or without other natural enzymes;
b) fermented by the action of yeast;
c) distilled (double or triple) in pot stills in such manner that the distillate has an aroma and taste derived from the materials used.

"Malt Irish Whiskey/ Irish Malt Whiskey" is made from natural raw materials, 100 % malted barley, water and yeast. Other natural enzymes may also be used at the brewing and fermentation stage. Malted barley is produced to individual specification by dedicated malting companies, which may be un-peated or peated in character. By using 100 % malted barley, "Malt Irish Whiskey/ Irish Malt

Whiskey" has distinctive smooth, velvet, full and oily texture with a malty and sweet taste. The Whisky must be:

a) saccharified by the diastase of malt contained therein, with or without other natural enzymes;
b) fermented by the action of yeast;
c) distilled (double or triple) in pot stills in such manner that the distillate has an aroma and taste derived from the materials used.

"Grain Irish Whiskey/Irish Grain Whiskey" is produced from malted barley (not exceeding 30 %) and includes whole unmalted cereals, usually maize, wheat or barley. Other natural enzymes may be used at the brewing and the fermentation stage. The Whisky must be:

a) saccharified by the diastase of malt contained therein, with or without other natural enzymes;
b) fermented by the action of yeast;
c) distilled (usually triple) in column stills in such manner that the distillate has an aroma and taste derived from the materials used and the column distillation method.

REFERENCES

http://faolex.fao.org/docs/pdf/eur77326.pdf

http://www.legislation.gov.uk/uksi/2008/3206/pdfs/uksi_20083206_en.pdf.

4

RAW MATERIALS

The raw materials from which a distiller can make alcohol are limited only by one's imagination. If the product has fermentable sugars in it, it will make alcohol.

Wine grapes, fruits, sugar cane, molasses, potato, wheat, corn, barley, rye, millet, sorghum, oats, triticale, lentil and quinoa are all examples of raw materials that can be used to create alcohol.

Botanicals such as Juniper, Coriander, Orange Peel, Lemon Peel, Lavender, Grains of Paradise, Angelica Root, Cinnamon are but some of the botanical materials that a distiller can use in flavoring Gin.

GRAPES, FRUIT, CANE & BEET

Wine grapes and fruit: when considering wine grapes and fruits as possible raw materials, an understanding of their basic chemistry is an essential starting point. One of the essential building blocks of grapes and fruit is the glucose molecule, $C_6H_{12}O_6$. Figure 2 illustrates the glucose molecule assemblage which comprises six Carbon atoms, twelve Hydrogen atoms and six Oxygen atoms. Chemists have system for numbering the atoms that make up molecules. Look at the right side of the molecule in Figure 2. The Carbon atom at right is Carbon atom number one, the Oxygen atom at right is number one and the two Hydrogen atoms are number one and two respectively. Now progress around this ring-like structure in a clock-wise fashion counting incrementally as you go. This numbering system will be useful when it comes to considering the subject of starch.

Glucose can be thought of a nature's fuel. Our bodies use glucose to create energy to fuel our muscles and our brains. Yeast cells also use glucose to create alcohol through a process called the *Embden Meyerhoff Parnas Glycolitic Pathway* which we shall discuss shortly.

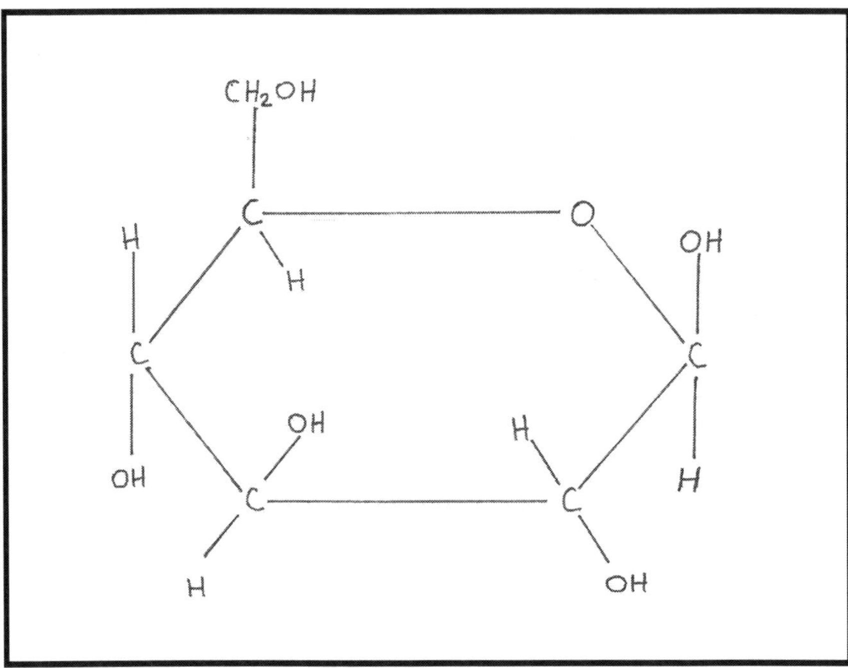

Figure 2 glucose molecule assemblage

In wine grapes and fruits, glucose molecules chemically bond to fructose molecules. Fructose is also $C_6H_{12}O_6$, but the chemical links between the atoms are slightly different than in glucose. Glucose and fructose will join together after each gives up a Hydrogen ion. The resulting combination of glucose and fructose is what is called a *sucrose* molecule. When we bite into a ripe piece of fruit and taste its sweet goodness, we are tasting sucrose. Figure 3 illustrates the sucrose molecular assemblage. As fruit ripens further, the Oxygen bond between the two molecules breaks down and yeast will then be able to consume each molecule individually.

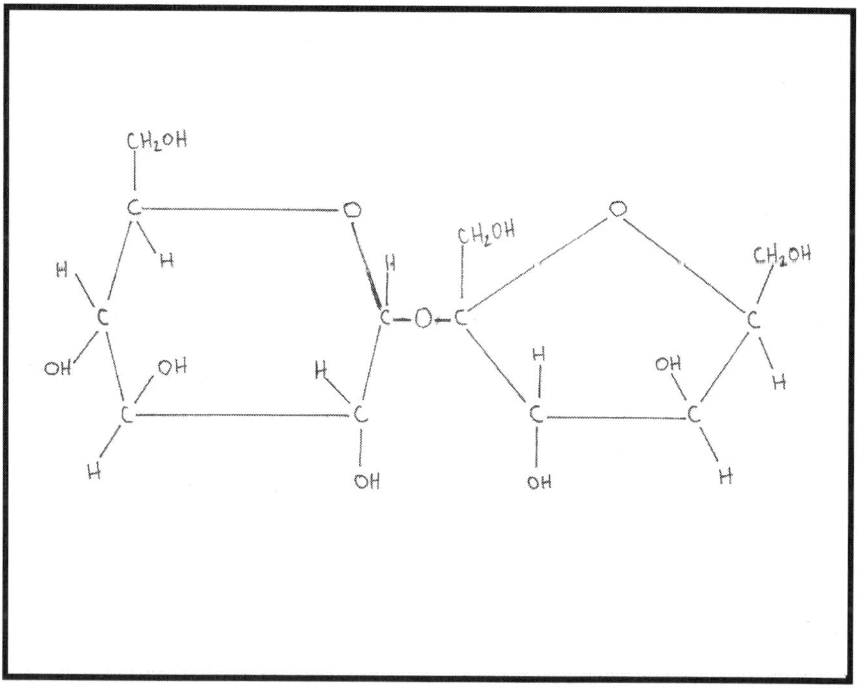

Figure 3 sucrose molecule assemblage

Fruits contain between 5% and 12% sugar by weight, with sugar comprising glucose, fructose and sucrose. The apparent wide variation in sugar content amongst fruits is a function of the type of fruit, the soil and climate as well as the seasonal growing conditions. Apples contain about 12 % sugar, apricots about 9 % sugar, blueberries about 7 % sugar, cherries about 11 % sugar, mangoes about 14 % sugar, papayas about 8 % sugar, peaches about 8 % and plums about 10 % sugar. Wine grapes have higher sugar content than fruits. Scientific literature suggests that wine grapes on average will contain about 18 % sugar. The type of grape, the climate and seasonal factors all will play a role in determining sugar content.

Sugar Cane: the basic chemistry of fruits and wine grapes also extends into an examination of sugar cane and its by-products. Sugar cane grows between north latitude 37 degrees and south latitude 31 degrees at altitudes up to no more than 1,000 meters provided such areas have significant rainfall and temperatures that range from 25 to 35 degrees C. To illustrate this geographic range, picture the entire globe with a horizontal line drawn through the southern tip of Italy and another horizontal line drawn through the southern tip of Africa. The areas around the world that fall between these lines are potential sugar cane growing regions provided they meet the elevation, rainfall and temperature parameters listed above.

After sugar cane is harvested it is taken to a processing plant where the canes are fed between rollers that press the juice out of the canes. The juice is then cooked in the presence of various chemicals to precipitate out sugar crystals. The remaining sludge at the end of this sugar extraction process is termed molasses. It still has residual sugars in it along with a fairly high concentration of minerals.

A tablespoon of molasses can provide the average person with up to 20 % of their daily mineral requirement. The sugar content of molasses (sucrose, glucose and fructose) is about 50 % which means molasses is a valuable raw material for distillers to use. Molasses can also contain bacteria strains such as *Leuconostoc Meserentoides* and *Zymomonas Mobilus.* Both can be detrimental to yeast during the fermentation process so it is imperative that distillers add yeast nutrients to a fermentation involving molasses.

If you are in a geographic location where you have ready access to sugar cane juice, it will have about 13 % sugar content. Small scale distillers in places like Brazil often produce a local spirit called *Cachaca* from fermented cane juice.

Sugar Beet: In parts of western Canada and neighboring American states like Montana, sugar beet is a common crop. The harvested sugar beets are cleaned, cut and heated in water to about 70C. The resulting sugary sweet liquid is further cooked in the presence of chemicals such as lime to precipitate out sugar crystals. The remaining sludge at the end of the process is too called a molasses, but it differs in taste and viscosity from Molasses left over from sugar cane processing. I know several home distillers that have made very credible tasting spirits from sugar beet molasses. My personal experience using the stuff has been very favorable also. Due to the reduced sugar content of sugar beet Molasses, I have found the addition of some cane sugar to be necessary in order to achieve decent alcohol yields. My basic recipe uses 60 % sugar beet molasses and 40 % cane sugar.

MALTED & UNMALTED GRAINS

Cereal Grain: when considering cereal grain as a raw material for alcohol creation, an examination of chemistry is again in order. Grain, consists mainly of proteins and carbohydrates with a small amount of fatty acid. The proteins are present in the outer part of the grain kernel in the form of the husk and the bran. Proteins are also present in the interior of the kernel. Think of the interior of a grain kernel as a webbed matrix of protein. Inside the various compartments of this webbed matrix are globules of starch, all tightly held in place by the matrix. Figure 4 illustrates the structure of a grain kernel.

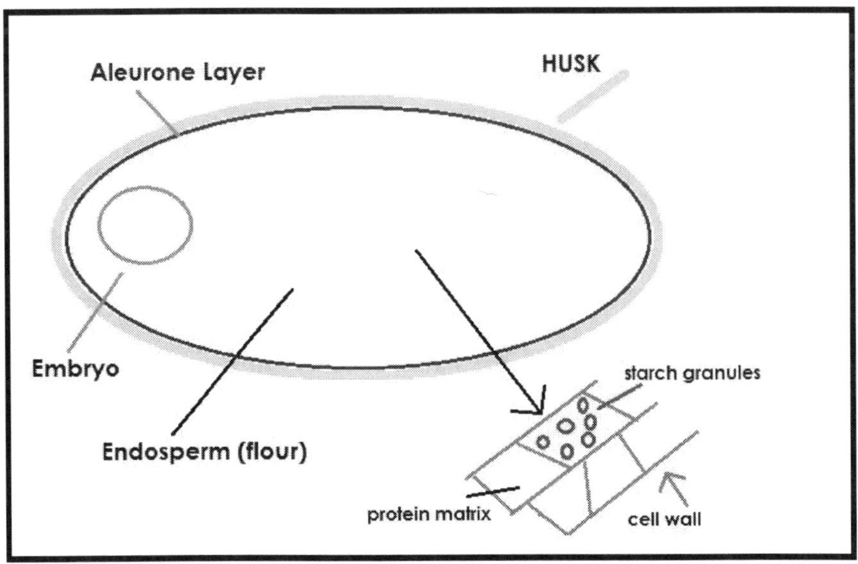

Figure 4 The structure of a grain kernel

To understand carbohydrate, one must return to a consideration of glucose, $C_6H_{12}O_6$. Take two glucose molecules and join them together and you have what is termed a *maltose*. Take three glucose molecules and join them together and you have what is termed a *maltotriose*. Take many glucose molecules and join them together and you have what is termed a *starch*. In our everyday language, we often call starch a carbohydrate or 'carbs'.

When using fruits, wine grapes or molasses as a raw material to create alcohol, the yeast cells are capable of digesting the glucose and fructose molecules. With a grain, yeast is not capable of digesting the long molecular chains of starch. In order to create alcohol from grain, the distiller must first break down the chains of starch into smaller building blocks – glucose, maltose and maltotriose. This is accomplished through the use of heat energy and *enzymes*.

An enzyme is a protein substance that hastens a chemical process or reaction. The enzyme itself is not destroyed or altered during its use.

Think back to your experience in your garden or perhaps your experience working around a farm. In the spring of the year when a seed is planted in the ground, it soon sprouts and up from the soil emerges a shoot. Anchored into the soil will be a root. When a kernel of grain is exposed to moisture and to warmth, it has sufficient intelligence to sense that it is time to grow. The grain kernel will generate a hormone called *giberellic acid*, sometimes called gibberelin. This hormone will find its way to the outer layer of the grain called the *aleurone layer*. Proteins are synthesized by this hormone to produce *alpha-amylase*, *beta-amylase* and a small amount of *limit dextrinase*. These three products are enzymes. These enzymes then proceed to assist the grain kernel by starting to nibble away at the globules of starch bound up inside the protein matrix of the kernel. The enzymes nibble away until they have produced glucose, maltose and maltotriose molecules.

These units are sugars and sugar is energy. This energy is then what assists the *embryo* in the grain kernel to send forth a root and a shoot. The root anchors itself into the soil. The shoot heads upwards in search of sunlight. The process of photosynthesis then takes over and a new cycle of growth gets underway resulting in a new crop for the farmer or a new harvest of vegetables for the gardener.

As distillers, we are neither farmers nor gardeners. We simply want to convert the chains of starch in the grain into smaller units that will be digestible by yeast. This then opens the door for a discussion of malting.

Malted Grain: when a farmer plants a seed of grain in his soil, the seed sends forth a root and a shoot. In other words, the kernel of grain sprouts. The industry term for this sprouting is *malting*. There are malting companies around the globe that cater specifically to the distilling and brewing industry by providing malted grains. Names like Cargill, Gambrinus, Great Western, Rahr, Malteurop, Boortmalt,

Castle and Briess are some of the names you might encounter on the world market.

Grain to be sold to a malting company must meet rigid criteria. The kernels must be plump, the total Nitrogen content of the grain must be low and the germinative capacity (the ability to generate a shoot quickly) must be high. A farmer who produces a crop of grain meeting these criteria stands to gain additional revenue for his grain if it is selected for use by a malting company.

Upon receipt at the malting plant, the grain kernels are cleaned to remove any dirt, debris and unwanted matter. The kernels are then exposed to moisture and dried repeatedly in cyclical fashion. The kernels soon develop a root and a shoot because the kernel senses the warmth and the moisture much as it would if it were planted in the soil of a farmer's field. But, here is where the malting process differs from what goes on in a farm field. As the root and shoot start to form and grow, the grain kernels are exposed to a gentle heat to bring a halt to this growth process. The heat causes the enzymes to stop working and essentially go to sleep. Malting companies have also discovered that it is possible at this stage to introduce some smoke to the process. The smoke molecules will adsorb onto the surface of the grain kernels. The next time you are savoring that smoky, peaty aroma in a single malt Scotch, think about the malting process and the addition of smoke from burning peat. With the enzymatic action put to sleep, the malting company will next tumble the grains to knock off the brittle root and shoot. The malted grain is then dried, weighed, bagged and shipped off to a brewing company or a distillery. One craft distillery that has taken smoking to a new level is Santa Fe Spirits in Santa Fe, New Mexico. Through an arrangement with Briess Malting, this distilling company was able to obtain mesquite wood-smoked barley. The flavors and aromas of the mesquite smoke are richly evident in its Colkegan Malt Whisky.

Mashing: when the distiller receives the shipment of malted grain, there are several steps that still must be executed in order to render the grain suitable to create alcohol.

The grain is first passed through a roller mill comprised of two or more cylindrical rollers with rough surfaces. The roller mill is designed so that one of the rollers turns at slightly higher speed than the other. The kernels of grain passing between the two rollers are then sheared apart.

Another option used by some distillers is that of a hammer mill. A hammer mill consists of a shaft that rotates at high speed. Attached to the shaft are hardened pieces of metal called hammers. The action of the grain kernels hitting the hammers causes the kernels to shatter. Different rotation speeds and different hammer configurations can create finer or coarser grain particles as the end user wishes.

The resulting material from either a roller mill or a hammer mill is termed a *grist.* The grist is next loaded into a vessel called a *mash tank.* (Note that in the beer industry a similar vessel called a mash tun will be employed). While it is true that the makers of Scotch Whisky do employ mash tuns as well, such practice is not commonplace among craft distillers or home distillers in North America. Water is then added to the grist and heat is imparted to the mash tank. Some distillers will employ hot steam injected right into the mash tank while others will have mash tanks with steam jackets built into the bottom portion of the tank. When the temperature of the grist/water mixture reaches 62C, something very important happens. The enzymes that had previously been put to sleep by the malting company come awake again. They pick up right where they left off – nibbling away at the starch molecules. But, this time the enzymes have an added benefit for the temperature range around 62-64C is the *gelatinization point* of grain. The gelatinization point of grain is that temperature where the kernels of grain structurally break down and the protein matrix that holds the globules of starch dissolves to free up the starch globules.

At this point, a deeper discussion of starch structure is important. Nature likes variety and with starches, nature provides us with long linear chains of starch, termed *amyloses.* Nature also provides us with complex branched structures called *amylopectins.* Approximately 30 % of the starch in grain consists of amylose with 70 % comprising amylopectin. Recall earlier in this chapter that glucose molecules have a numbering nomenclature. If two glucose molecules are joined so that Carbon atom number one and Carbon atom number four are in close proximity, this is what is termed an *alpha 1,4 linkage.* If Carbon atom number one and Carbon atom number six are in close proximity, this is termed an *alpha 1,6 linkage.* Figure 5 illustrates these linkages.

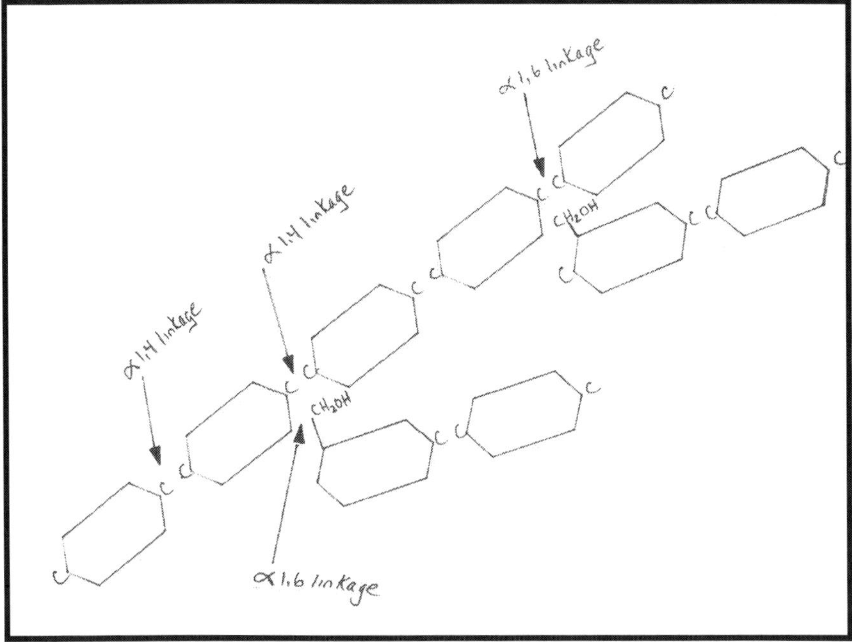

Figure 5 alpha 1,4 and 1,6 linkages in starch chains

With the grain kernels gelatinized and the starches freed from their captivity inside the protein matrix in the grain kernels, the enzymes can start attacking the starch chains.

At the 62-64C temperature level, the beta-amylase enzyme is operating at its most efficient. It attacks loose ends of the starch chains, nibbling off units of two and three glucose units (maltose and maltotriose respectively). Beta-amylase is sometimes referred to as an exo-enzyme for its inherent ability to attack starches from the ends.

At the 62-64C temperature level, the alpha-amylase enzyme is also active, but it is not operating at peak efficiency. The alpha-amylase enzymes are busy attacking the linear amylose chains, cutting them at the 1,4 linkages. As the amylose chains are cut, this creates more loose ends for the beta-amylase to feast on. Alpha-amylase is often called an endo-enzyme for its ability to attack starches in the mid-chain portion.

After a 20-30 minute hold time at 62-64C, the distiller will then add more heat to the mash tank and raise the temperature to 72-74C. At this temperature, the activity of the beta-amylase is reduced significantly, but the alpha-amylase kicks into high gear and continues attacking the 1,4 linkage sites.

After 20-30 minutes at this temperature level, the starch chains have been pretty much ripped apart into smaller units – sugars. What remains is the 1,6 linkage sites which neither alpha or beta amylase can completely contend with. The un-broken 1,6 linkage sites are termed *dextrins* and are what give beer its sweet, mouthfeel that make your tastebuds cry out for more.

As distillers, we are not interested in mouthfeel or any remaining dextrins. This is why many distillers yeasts will come pre-mixed with a small amount of *amyloglucosidase* (or AG for short) in them. AG is an enzyme that functions at normal fermentation temperatures and is designed to attack and tear apart the glucose molecules at the 1,6 linkage sites.

Summing up, then, with fruits, molasses and wine grapes, it was noted that yeast would be able to generate alcohol by digesting the sugars present. With grains, we have to first employ heat and enzymes to tear down the starches into smaller units of sugar so that the yeast can generate alcohol.

Un-Malted Grain: what if a distiller wants to use un-malted grains instead of the more expensive malted grains? Where do the enzymes come from? The answer is, the distiller will use artificial, man-made enzymes.

Distillers can realize significant cost savings by sourcing grain directly from a grain farmer. It is advisable, though, to first have a look at a sample of the grain that is for sale. Examine the kernels closely for evidence of dark staining which is a sign of mold and bacteria that will be harmful to yeast during the fermentation process.

In my experience, I have had excellent luck sourcing grain from a Certified Seed Grower. Seed growers are carefully regulated by government agencies and will not sell a sub-standard grain product. In addition, seed-quality grain has been passed through a cleaning plant so the grain will be free of dirt, debris and weed seeds.

When using un-malted grains, it is still necessary to pass the grain through a roller mill or a hammer mill. The resulting grist is then loaded into a mash tank along with water. An un-malted grain will have a higher gelatinization temperature than a malted grain. The distiller will heat the mash tank and its contents to as high as 90C in order to break down the structure of the crushed grain kernels.

At this temperature, a high temperature tolerant artificial enzyme will be added to the mash. The mash will then be held at the 90C level for perhaps up to 60 minutes. Each enzyme manufacturer will have a different recommended temperature and time.

The mash will then be allowed to cool down to somewhere around 65C as recommended by the enzyme maker. At this point a second enzyme will be added. The mash will be held at this temperature level for a specified period of time.

After allowing the mash to cool to around 55C, a third enzyme will be added.

These artificial, man-made enzymes are all synthesized from naturally occurring bacteria and fungus. The significant differences between using malted grain and its naturally developed alpha and beta amylase enzymes and an artificial enzymes are primarily time and temperature. Artificial enzymes will demand a higher mash temperature and the overall time required to complete the breakdown of the starch chains to smaller sugar units will be perhaps three times as long.

I have been using artificial enzymes from companies such as White Labs (USA), Enzymash (USA) and Novozymes (USA) with great success. I recently was introduced to a new enzyme maker, BSG Canada. I am quite pleased with their products and regularly use their enzymes when demonstrating small scale mashes in front of Workshop participants. Take the time to talk to these various suppliers. They are there to help you and you will find they are extremely knowledgeable.

YIELD

Theoretical Yields: the question then arises – how much alcohol can one expect to get from grain as compared to fruits, grapes or molasses. To address this question, we turn to a discussion of theoretical yield.

100 kgs of good quality Corn will in theory provide about 45 liters of alcohol.

100 kgs of good quality Soft White Wheat will provide about 42 liters of alcohol.

100 kgs of good quality Hard Winter Wheat will provide about 44 liters of alcohol.

100 kgs of good quality Rye will provide about 42 liters of alcohol.

100 kgs of good quality Barley will provide about 42 liters of alcohol.

100 kgs of Potato will provide between 8 and 13 liters of alcohol. The species of potato will be the major determinant in the starch content. For example Idaho (Russet) potatoes have a higher starch content than Yukon Gold potatoes. The higher starch content of Idaho potatoes makes them ideal candidates for oven roasting. Yukon Gold potatoes with their lower starch content are ideal for traditional mashed potato dishes. The point, however, is that potatoes have a markedly lower starch content than grains. If you are intent on using potato as a raw material for making alcohol, you will have to source the potato for an extremely low cost in order to maintain some semblance of profitable economics. This explains why one does not see a lot of Potato Vodka on the liquor store shelves.

Earlier in this chapter, the average sugar content of various Fruits was briefly discussed. Recall that:

100 kgs of good quality Plums will yield about 5 liters of alcohol.

100 kgs of good quality Peaches will yield about 4.5 liters of alcohol.

100 kgs of good quality Papaya will yield about 4.5 liters of alcohol.

100 kgs of good quality Mangoes will yield about 9 liters of alcohol.

100 kgs of good quality Apple will yield about 7.75 liters of alcohol.

100 kgs of good quality Apricots will yield about 6 liters of alcohol.

100 kgs of good quality Blueberries will yield about 4 liters of alcohol.

100 kgs of good quality Cherries will yield about 6 liters of alcohol.

100 kgs of good quality Wine grapes will yield about 10 liters of alcohol.

100 kgs of good quality Molasses will yield about 32 liters of alcohol.

Theoretical Yield Calculations: to understand how these theoretical yields are arrived at we must go back to the mid-1800s and to the work of French scientist Joseph Louis Gay-Lussac. Gay-Lussac was a pioneer in quantifying how sugars in the presence of yeast could create alcohol. Gay-Lussac's legacy to the world of distillation was the now famous Gay-Lussac equation:

$$\text{Sugar} + \text{Yeast} = \text{Alcohol} + CO_2$$

Expressed in chemical equation format, the Gay-Lussac equation is:

$$C_6H_{12}O_6 + \text{Yeast} = 2\ C_6H_5OH + 2\ CO_2$$

Next one must turn to the Periodic Table of the Elements and those distant memories of college and university chemistry class. The

Periodic Table details data such as atomic number and gram molecular weight for the elements that comprise our known world.

From the Periodic Table of Elements, note that Carbon has a gram molecular weight of 12.01 grams per mole, Hydrogen a gram molecular weight of 1.007 gram per mole and Oxygen a gram molecular weight of 15.999 grams per mole. A mole (sometimes abbreviated mol) is defined by international chemistry regulatory bodies as that amount of material that contains as many atoms as there are in 12 grams of the isotope carbon C^{12}. This number of atoms in Carbon C^{12} is expressed by the Avogadro constant 6.022 x $10^{23.}$ I am sure that had my engineering school professor's told me that someday I would be using this stuff to help me make better Whisky, I would have paid better attention!

In other words, 6.022 x 10^{23} atoms of Carbon will weigh 12.01 grams. A like number of Hydrogen atoms will weigh 1.007 gram and a like number of Oxygen atoms will weigh 15.999 grams.

Knowing the gram molecular weights of Carbon, Hydrogen and Oxygen, one can quickly calculate the molecular weights of sugar, alcohol and carbon dioxide in the Gay-Lussac equation.

A molecule of $C_6H_{12}O_6$ has a molecular weight of 180.13. The two molecules of C_6H_5OH have a molecular weight of 92.12 and the two molecules of CO_2 have a molecular weight of 88.01.

Dividing the molecular weight of the 2 molecules of alcohol by the molecular weight of the sugar molecule yields 92.12/180.13 = 0.511

The general formula for density states that density = mass/volume.

The density of alcohol at 20C is 0.79 kgs per liter.

Consider this example. Take 100 kgs of Hard Winter Wheat with a starch content of 70 %. Assuming this starch all gets broken down into smaller units of glucose and all of that glucose ferments to produce alcohol and carbon dioxide, we can refer back to the Gay-Lussac equation. The 100 kgs of Wheat will deliver 70 kgs of fermentable sugar. Multiplying this figure by 0.511 from the Gay-Lussac equation yields 70 x 0.511 = 35.77. That is, this amount of fermentable sugar will yield 35.77 kgs of alcohol. Inserting this figure into the general expression for density yields 35.77/0.79 = 45.27 liters of alcohol. Thus, we say that the theoretical yield of 100 kgs of Hard Winter Wheat with a starch content of 70 % is 45.27 liters of alcohol.

Consider one more example, this time using fruit.

Take 100 kgs of good quality Apples with a sugar content of 12 %. Assuming this sugar ferments to produce alcohol and carbon dioxide, we can refer back to the Gay-Lussac equation. The 100 kgs of apple will deliver 12 kgs of fermentable sugar. Multiplying this figure by 0.511 from the Gay-Lussac equation yields 12 x 0.511 = 6.12. That is, this amount of fermentable sugar will yield 6.12 kgs of alcohol. Inserting this figure into the general expression for density yields 6.12/0.79 = 7.75 liters of alcohol. Thus we say that the theoretical yield of 100 kgs of good quality Apples with a sugar content of 12 % is 7.75 liters of alcohol.

THE ALWAYS CONTENTIOUS NGS

Neutral Grain Spirits: what if a distiller did not wish to use Grains, Fruits, or Molasses? This leads to a discussion of the very sensitive issue of Neutral Grain Spirits.

In Ontario, Canada there is a company called Commercial Alcohols Ltd. This organization owns four large scale ethanol distilleries where is produces 95 % alcohol (called NGS or GNS) using a feedstock of Corn.

Most of this alcohol is destined for the gasoline producers who blend up to 10 % of it into their gasoline brands for motor vehicles. In America, there are companies such as Cargill and MGP Ingredients who have similar ethanol distilleries. A craft distiller can purchase this grain alcohol from these vendors at around the $5.00 per liter price point (Canadian funds). This alcohol can then be passed through a still at a craft distillery to produce Vodka or possibly even a Gin.
The benefit of using Neutral Grain Spirits is that the craft distiller does not need to spend the up-front capital dollars to buy a mash tank and fermenter tanks.
The significant downside to using Grain Spirits is the lack of craftsmanship involved. I am a purist. Some would even say I am a snob. I believe that a craft distiller should be making alcohol from raw materials and not buying ready-made alcohol from a large corporation. A case in point is Lucky Bastard Distilling in Saskatoon, Canada. It irks me to no end to see their over-priced Vodka on liquor store shelves when I know it was made from someone else's Neutral Grain Spirits.

BOTANICALS

Gin Botanicals: there are a myriad of botanical raw materials available to a distiller seeking to make Gin.

Juniper: one botanical that must be present in Gin is Juniper. However, the legislation does not stipulate how much Juniper. Juniper is actually a berry and is a member of the cypress family of plants. The earliest mention of Juniper in literature goes back to 1266 and reference to a remedy for stomach pain. Most Juniper grows in places like Italy and eastern Europe. However, it does grow in limited quantity in many parts of North America. Take a drive through New

Mexico, USA at the right time of year and you will see juniper shrubs bearing small purplish berries. I recently learned that Juniper even grows in the western Canadian Provinces. Although I am told these berries are very pungent. Shop around for Juniper. Try berries from different locations. Maybe even try blending different Juniper berries to impart a completely unique taste profile to your Gin. The molecules present in Juniper that impart its unique flavors include *alpha-pinene, myrcene* and *limonene.*

Coriander: the second most important flavoring botanical in Gin is the coriander seed. Coriander plants grow in many parts of the world and will be easily obtainable. The leaf of the coriander plant is called cilantro. The essential oils in coriander seeds include *linalool, thymol* and *geranyl acetate.* Collectively, these oils impart slight woodsy, floral and citrus notes to Gin.

Lemon Peel: lemon peel will be available in dried form. The best lemon peel for Gin making will have originated in the Mediterranean region. A small amount of lemon peel will give Gin a fresh, citrus note.

Orange Peel: orange peel will likewise be available in dried form. The best orange peel for Gin making will come from Spain. As you source orange peel you will find it will be available in bitter and sweet varieties. Experiment with each type and decide which you prefer. I have had Gin made with just sweet orange peel and I have had Gin with both sweet and bitter peel. The difference is slight, but there is a difference. Another peel worth investigating is from the Italian Solerno Blood Orange.

Angelica Root: angelica root comes from Germany and Belgium. Angelica has a reputation for imparting a floral note to Gin. In fact, Angelica is a close relative of the parsley and dill plants. I personally do not use angelica root in my home-made Gins, but research shows that many of the big commercial names in Gin do use angelica root. The essential oils in angelica include *limonene, pinene* and *beta-phellandrene.*

Orris Root: this is the root bulb of the iris flower plant. Mention of this root goes back to Greek and Roman times when it was highly prized for use in perfumes. It has a reputation in Gin circles as being the 'fixer". That is, the active ingredient, *irone*, reportedly marries and holds together the tastes and aromas from the various botanicals in a Gin.

Cinnamon: cinnamon is the bark of a tree native to the island of modern-day Sri Lanka. Today much cinnamon comes from India and Brazil. Cinnamon is high in chemical compounds *eugenol, cinnamaldehyde* and *linaool.*

Cassia: Cassia is a relative of the cinnamon family and originates in south-east Asia, hence its colloquial name 'Chinese cinnamon'. Like Cinnamon, it will add a spicy, floral note to a Gin.

Cardamom: if you dabble in Indian cooking or if you frequent Indian restaurants, you have seen Cardamom pods and the tiny black seeds in the pods. Cardamom is a member of the ginger family. In small quantity it can add a spicy, citrus type note to a Gin. The essential oils in Cardamom include *linalool* and *linalyl acetate.*

Grains of Paradise: these small dark brown berries from West Africa resemble small peppercorns and are a member of the ginger family. They impart a peppery note to a Gin if used in small quantity. Grains of Paradise is a key ingredient in *Bombay Sapphire Gin.*

Star Anise: this eight segment, star-shaped seed comes from an evergreen tree (related to the magnolia) that grows in southwest China and parts of Vietnam. In a Gin, star anise will impart a very definite licorice taste. Active ingredients in Star Anise include *anethole* and *glycyrrhizin.*

Cubeb: we are all familiar with Cubeb's relative – black pepper. The *piperene* and *limonene* essential oils will give Gin a spicy, citrus note.

Fruits: I have had Gin where small quantities of Blueberry and even Rhubarb have been added. It is hard to detect these individual fruit notes in the Gin on a stand-alone basis, but they are nonetheless there combined with the other botanicals and imparting subtle notes of flavor to the Gin.

Flowers: I have had Gin containing flowers petals from the high desert around Santa Fe, New Mexico. I have had Gin containing flower petals from marigold flowers grown in western Canada. The use of flowers is an open book. Experiment and see what happens.

I regard Gin as a blank artistic canvas with the distiller as the artist. The days of Gin all tasting pretty much the same are over thanks to the craft distilling movement. Explore, investigate and experiment. You will have a lot of fun with Gin.

THE UNUSUAL

Lactose: lastly, there is one unusual raw material that deserves only brief mention – for you may never encounter it. I am referring to lactose, or milk sugar. When a cheesemaker sets about making cheese, an enzyme substance called *rennet* is added to the milk. The rennet causes the proteins in the milk to separate into *curds* and *whey.* The curds are collected for cheese and the remaining whey liquid is sold to a food processing company. Whey will contain about 5 % lactose sugar which is comprised of a glucose molecule joined to a galactose molecule. The food processor will extract the lactose and sell it to companies for use as a sweetener. Brewers know how to utilize lactose. It is apparently one of the ingredients that give Guinness beer its silky sweetness. With distilling, the standard *saccharomyces cerevisiae* yeast cannot thoroughly digest the glucose-galactose combined molecule. But, lately, scientists have figured out how to use a special yeast called *kluyveromyces marxianus* to ferment lactose. Distillation of the fermented lactose alcohol seems to be getting the name *alpha-Vodka* in craft distilling circles. Rheault Distilling in Ontario, Canada apparently uses lactose-based alcohol in making its *Loon Vodka.* Leche Spirits of Roswell, New Mexico launched its *Milk Money Vodka* in 2015 complete with a bottle that resembles an old-fashioned milk bottle.

REFERENCES

The Malt Academy has a very excellent YouTube video on line that illustrates the malting process. (https://youtu.be/BeKD9x7nMg8)

A German firm called Kaspar-Schulz Brew Systems manufactures brewing equipment and also small in-house malting plants. They have an excellent YouTube video on line that further illustrates the malting process. (https://youtu.be/I_VLw8Ih8zQ)

www.comalc.com
www.cargillfoods.com
www.mgpingredients.com
http://secure.herbies-herbs.com
http://www.starwest-botanicals.com

Whisky: Technology, Production and Marketing, Production of American Whiskies, R. Ralph, Ch 19., Elsevier Press, 2003, USA.

Fermented Beverage Production, second edition, edited by Andrew G.H.

Lea, John R. Piggott, chapter 13, Vodka, Gin and Other Flavored Spirits, R.I. Aylott, Kluwer Academic Press, 2003, USA.

Fermented Beverage Production, second edition, edited by Andrew G.H. Lea, John R. Piggott, chapter 16, Production of Heavy and Light Rums, R.Piggot, Kluwer Academic Press, 2003, USA.

Fermented Beverage Production, first edition, edited by Andrew G.H. Lea, John R. Piggott, chapter 1, Production of Fermentable Extracts from Cereals and Fruits, A. Paterson, J. Swanston, J. Piggot, Springer Press, 1995, USA.

The Manufacture of Scotch Grain Whisky, Magnus Pyke, Journal of the Institute of Brewing, Volume 71, Issue 3, pages 209–218, May-June 1965.

The Drunken Botanist, Amy Stewart, Algonquin Books of Chapel Hill, 2013, USA.

5

YEAST & FERMENTATION

THE FRIENDLY FUNGUS

Yeast is a member of the fungus family. It is a uni-cellular organism about 1/10th the diameter of a human hair. Under a microscope, it takes the 400X magnification setting to be able to view a yeast cell.

As pointed out in a previous chapter, early mankind understood that there was an organism of sorts that would make fruit and grapes ferment to generate a liquid capable of imparting a pleasant intoxicated feeling.

Following the refinement of the microscope in the mid-1800s, a basic understanding of yeast was advanced by scientists such as Louis Pasteur. Prior to Pasteur, it was thought that sugar merely touching yeast would generate fermentation. Pasteur was the first to prove that yeast was a living organism and that the process of fermentation was much more involved than had been previously thought. As microscope capability continued to advance, a deeper look inside a yeast cell became possible. Today, scientists have a very detailed understanding of what comprises a yeast cell.

Figure 6 illustrates what the interior of a yeast cell looks like. Scientists have now come to understand that the *cell wall* is comprised of proteins such as mannan and glucan. The *nucleus* is a storehouse of DNA material required for growth. The *vacuole* is a storehouse of nutrients and also an enzyme called *protease.* The *ribosomes* are responsible for synthesizing proteins and encoding DNA material essential for yeast re-production. The *mitrochondrion* can be thought of as the powerhouse of the yeast cell where energy is generated and where the entire cell cycle of growth through death is regulated. All of these working parts are contained in the *cytoplasm* which is made up of glycogen – a branched starch-type material. The cytoplasm is also home to a second enzyme called *invertase*. The invertase and protease enzymes work together to assist the yeast cell in absorbing sugar molecules through the cell wall.

A yeast cell reproduces itself by a process called *budding* in which it creates a daughter cell identical in appearance to itself. A normal, healthy yeast cell can create perhaps as many as 20 daughters, with each of these daughters then being able to create daughters of their own. Given the proper conditions, yeast cells can rapidly multiply and that is exactly what a brewer or distiller wants.

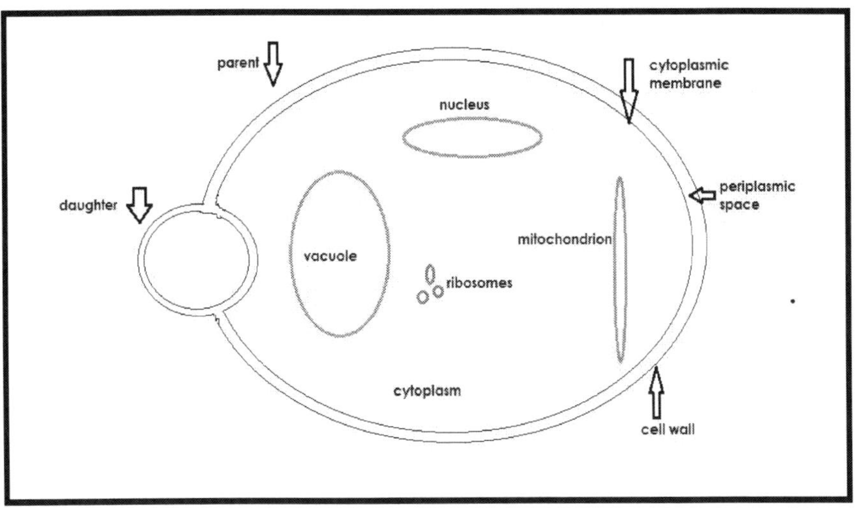

Figure 6 Inside a Yeast Cell

WHAT YEAST NEEDS

In order for yeast to properly reproduce, it needs proper pH, proper temperature, inorganic ions, vitamins, nitrogen, a carbon source and water. Let's examine these in turn.

Proper pH: pH is short form for Hydrogen Potential. Mathematically, pH is the negative base 10 logarithm of the number of moles per liter of Hydrogen ions in a solution. pH values are expressed on a scale that goes from 1 to 14. A solution that has pH 1 will have a high level of Hydrogen ions.

For example, H_3PO_4, phosphoric acid, will have a high level of Hydrogen ions and as such in concentrated form may have pH as low as 1. Caustic soda, NaOH. has fewer Hydrogen ions and mathematically, its pH might be near 14. The water that you and I drink from the tap in our kitchens will have a pH of about 7.

Proper Temperature: temperature is the one variable that will most certainly have a detrimental effect on yeast. Expose yeast to a temperature much above 34C and you will most certainly kill it. Yeast for distillers will function optimally between 20C and 30C, with each yeast manufacturer having a different optimal range. For example, yeast maker Lallemand says its yeast functions optimally at 28 to 30C. Allowing temperature to drift down to near 20C will not kill Lallemand yeast, but the rate of fermentation will slow markedly. White Labs on the other hand says that its yeast functions optimally at between 22 and 25C.

When adding yeast to a fermentation vessel, it is critical also not to shock the yeast. Prior to adding the yeast to the fermenter, take the yeast and add it to water that is at about 28C. Stir the dried yeast particles into the water to make a slurry. When you add this slurry to the fermenter full of grain mash, which will be at about 28-30C, the temperature differential between fermenter tank and yeast particles will only be a few degrees so no shock will occur. In the case of fruit or wine as a raw starting material, follow the manufacturers recommendations which will most likely call for the yeast slurry to be added at room temperature to the material in the fermenter.

As a ferment proceeds, it generates significant amounts of heat. This will be discussed further in a later chapter on equipment needed for distilling. But, for here and now, note that the amount of heat generated will be a function of the size of fermenter and its ability to retain heat. For my personal research and experimentation, I conduct my ferments in a 25 liter plastic fermenter pail purchased from my local home brewing store. Given its small volume, it conducts heat to its surroundings relatively quickly. Even though a small ferment like this might generate 6C of additional heat, I have not had a problem with yeast becoming stressed due to overheating. Compare this to a large 1200 liter tank with large amounts of grain or other raw material inside. The heat generated will be significant and this heat must be removed via cooling jackets on the tank otherwise yeast distress will surely result.

Inorganic Ions: to keep a yeast cell at its happiest, ideally it should be exposed to about 70 ppm Magnesium ions, 120 ppm Potassium ions, 0.3 ppm Zinc ions, 100-120 ppm Calcium ions, 0.15 ppm Manganese ions, 0.10 ppm Copper ions. Water in many parts of the globe will have ion contents close to these levels. Depending on where you live, you may have to make some modest additions of mineral salts. One very excellent resource to help you adjust water chemistry is the book *How to Brew* by author John Palmer.

Vitamins: just as humans function better if we receive a small amount of Vitamin B in our diets, so too does yeast function better. When starting a fermentation, it is advisable to add up between 200 and 400 ppm of a powdered yeast nutrient to your fermentation vessel. In a 25 liter fermentation, this equates to between 5 and 10 mls. I typically use a product such as Nutristart, made by French company Laffort. The vitamins in the powdered nutrient will give yeast what it needs to thrive. Not all powdered nutrients are created alike. Always check the manufacturer's recommended rates of addition first.

Nitrogen: yeast needs Nitrogen and it will get it from the raw materials used. Husk and bran material in grains for example have sufficient Nitrogen to keep yeast happy. Again, one may wish to add a powdered yeast nutrient at the start of a fermentation. These powdered nutrients contain di-ammonium phosphate (sometimes called DAP). Recall that the ammonium ion is NH_3^- and provides the source of Nitrogen to the yeast.

Carbon Source: as previously discussed, glucose with its six Carbon atoms is the basic building block of starches in grains. Glucose and fructose are present in Fruits, Grapes and Molasses. The Carbon atoms in these molecules provide the source of carbon for yeast.

Proper Storage: your supply of yeast should be stored in the refrigerator. At normal refrigerator temperatures, yeast will only lose 4% of its viability per year. Unrefrigerated yeast will lose about 20% of its viability per year.

Water: good quality water is critical for yeast to function. More about water in the next chapter.

HOW MUCH YEAST?

There is one more variable that is important and that is the quantity of yeast that is added to the fermentation vessel. Through discussions with White Labs (USA) and with Lallemand Yeast, I have determined that 9-10 grams of yeast per 20 liters of mash volume is the optimal pitching rate. The analogy that I like to use is that of a table laid out with all sorts of delicious sugary, sweet food. You have invited guests to this festive occasion. Think of these guests as yeast cells. If there are too many invited guests, there will not be enough food to go around and guests will be most unhappy. If there are too few invited guests, each guest will eat until fully contented, but there will be food left over. What a waste! If, however, an optimal number of guests are invited, all will feast until satisfied and all will be happy.

There are a few items that are absolutely toxic to yeast. These include fusarium molds, chlorine ions and iron ions. If sourcing grains from a farmer, be sure to visually inspect the grains for evidence of dark staining on the kernels – a sure sign of toxic molds. Be sure to also avoid farm-sourced grain that contains weeds, seeds and chaff. Yeast has been known to consume this foreign matter and generate alcoholic solvents which can ruin a distillation. If using Fruits, Wine grapes or even Molasses, be sure there are no visible signs of toxic molds. The water used as part of the fermentation must be free of iron ions and chlorine, both of which are toxic to yeast.

PHASES

The process of fermentation is best understood by breaking it into four distinct phases – Lag Phase, Exponential Phase, Stationary Phase and Decline Phase.

Lag Phase: when the distiller adds yeast to the fermenter, at first nothing appears to be happening. Hence the expression Lag Phase. But, there is something happening. The yeast is intelligent enough to realize that it is surrounded by material that it can use to reproduce itself. It begins absorbing Oxygen from the mash in the fermenter tank. It further absorbs nutrients and inorganic ions from the water and mash material in the tank. Academic literature suggests that the optimal amount of dissolved Oxygen in the material to be fermented is 10 ppm. Yeast also absorbs Nitrogen from the grain material in the fermenter and also from any powdered nutrient you have added to the fermenter. It uses this absorbed material to strengthen its cell walls in preparation for eventual fermentation. It uses the absorbed

Nitrogen material to bolster the enzymes *protease* and *invertase.*

Recall from an earlier discussion that enzymes are proteins that make a chemical process proceed smoothly and efficiently. The chemical process in the case of yeast will be the action of glucose, maltose, maltotriose and fructose molecules moving (absorbing) through the yeast cell wall. The enzymes make this process proceed smoothly.

Exponential Phase: with Oxygen and nutrients absorbed, the yeast cells can now quickly start generating daughter cells by way of the budding process. Those daughters will make then daughters of their own through the budding process. The increase in yeast cell population is extremely rapid. In fact, exponentially so. This is why this phase of the fermentation process is given the name Exponential Phase. It is also during this Exponential Phase that the process of fermentation gets underway.

Stationary Phase: with the Exponential Phase complete, the yeast cells have made all the daughter cells they can make. Cell growth rate then levels off – hence the expression Stationary Phase. Fermentation continues through the Stationary Phase.

This is where a distinction can be drawn between yeast cells and members of the plant and animal kingdoms. Plants and animals in the absence of Oxygen will simply die because they are *aerobic.* They need Oxygen to live. But, yeast is a survivor. Through time it has developed the ability to survive in the absence of Oxygen (*anaerobic*). When faced with a lack of Oxygen, yeast will start to look for sugars to eat. The point where yeast shifts from displaying aerobic behavior to anaerobic behavior is called the *Crabtree Effect*, named after English biochemist Herbert Crabtree.

As yeast starts to absorb sugars through its cell walls with the aid of the invertase and protease enymes, the *Embden Meyerhoff Parnas*

Glycolytic Pathway (EMP) process starts to unfold. This metabolic pathway first comprises a sequence of complex reactions that convert glucose to a molecule called *pyruvate*. Free energy compounds termed *ATP* and *NADH* are also formed.

Once the pyruvate has been formed, there are additional reactions that take place. Bacteria in the fermentation tank can react with pyruvate to form lactic acid. A complex series of reactions can take some pyruvate and convert it into propionate, acetate, acetone, butyrate, butanol, propanol and combinations/permutations thereof. But, if all goes well, a goodly amount of the pyruvate will convert to an acetaldehyde and thence to ethanol.

The EMP process also generates esters, acetates and aldehydes by way of amino acid synthesis and enzyme synthesis. These contribute significantly to the flavor of the fermented material. there is more than just the EMP process that generates alcohol.

Although details remain somewhat unclear to me, researchers Nykanen and Suomalainen in 1983 expressed the opinion that yeast is even capable of synthesizing the esters of the fatty acids contained in raw materials to create higher density alcohol molecules partly outside of the EMP process. The image in Figure 7 illustrates the EMP process.

As a distiller, it is not essential to have an intimate understanding of this process. Just understand that it is a complex series of reactions. If the yeast becomes stressed due to temperature, a lack of nutrient, a lack of available sugar to consume or any other reason, the entire EMP process will be upset and a reduced amount of ethanol will be generated. Reduced amounts of ethanol generated then have immediate effects on the economics of a distillery operation.

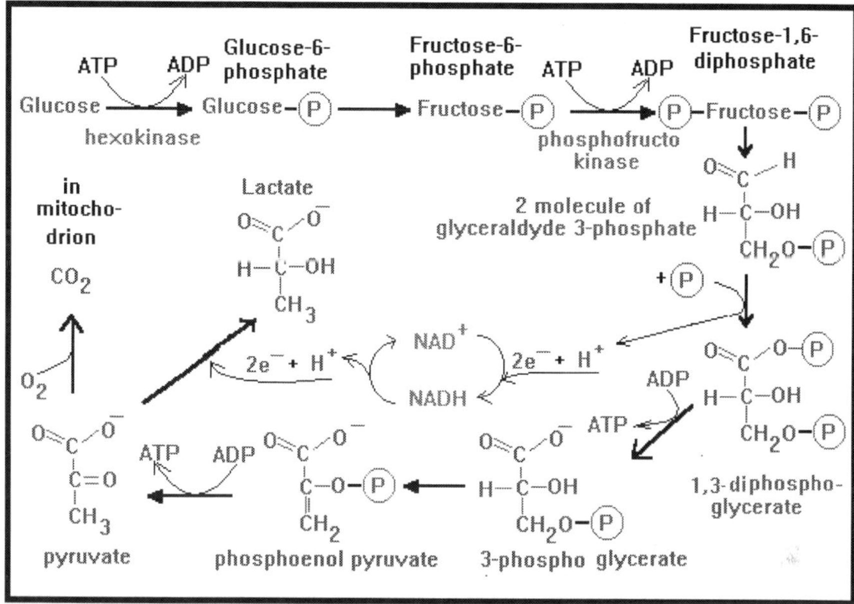

Figure 7 the EMP Process

Decline Phase: eventually, the yeast cells will run out of sugars to consume and at that point the population of cells will decline. This is called the Decline Phase as it signals the end of the fermentation cycle. The graph in Figure 8 illustrates the phases of the fermentation process with some typical times.

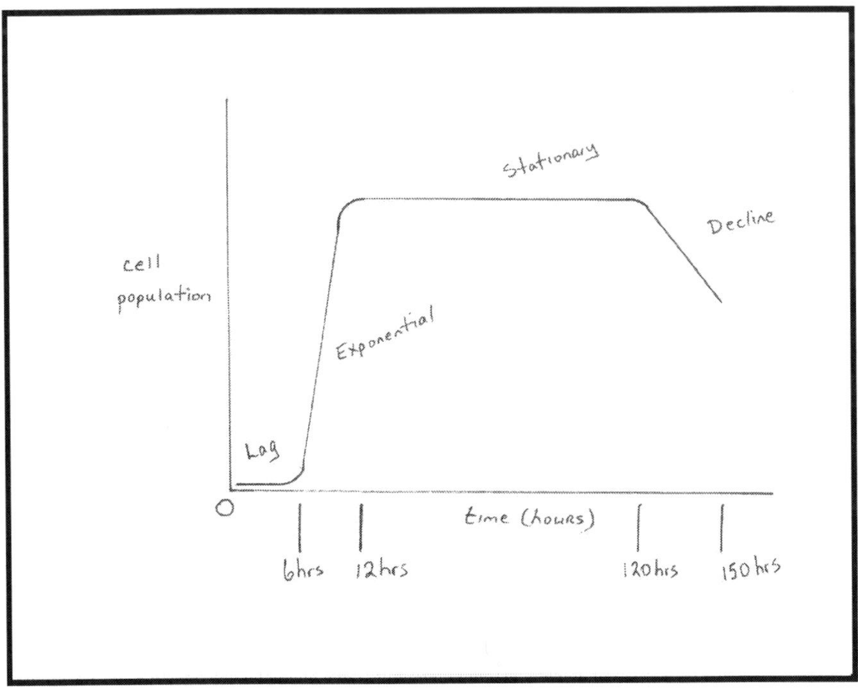

Figure 8 – Phases of the Fermentation Process

The EMP process reveals that the Gay-Lussac Equation referenced earlier greatly oversimplifies matters. According to the Gay-Lussac Equation, sugar in the presence of yeast will create ethanol and carbon dioxide. Such was the level of rudimentary understanding in the mid-1800s. The EMP process as we now know generates many different members of the alcohol family in addition to ethanol. The EMP process also generates heat energy.

STRAINS

Yeast Strains: one question that I am often asked pertains to the varieties of yeast available. Thanks to advances in genomic profiling in the 1990s, scientists now understand that the main species of yeast in nature is one called *saccharomyces cerevisiae.* But, under the umbrella of this species are nearly 700 different strains. The analogy I like to use is man's best friend – *canus familiaris,* otherwise called *dog.* Underneath the umbrella of canus familiaris are many strains. Think poodle, doberman, pit bull, boxer, hound, bulldog and so on. All have four legs, a tail and will bark.. But all are different and have different capabilities. And so it is with yeast - saccharomyces cerevisiae. There are yeasts that are ideally suited to making English ale, porter and stout. There are yeasts for red wines, white wines and champagnes. In the world of distilling, there are yeasts for Rum, Whisky and Vodka. There are all sorts of high alcohol tolerant Turbo Yeasts as well. I have had bad luck with these various Turbo Yeasts sold on the Internet. Participants from my Workshops have likewise had Turbo Yeast generate fermented mash that smells of a combination of stinky cheese and sweaty running shoes. Avoid Turbo Yeasts at all costs.

Also - be sure never to use a beer yeast to ferment a mash you have made for future alcohol production. Beer yeasts are engineered to deliver the 5-6% alcohol plus flavor that we normally associate with a beer. Distillers yeasts are engineered with additional fatty acids and nutrients in them to deliver a higher alcohol content. Remember, as distillers, we are not drinking the results of our fermentations. We will be passing that fermented material through a still to extract the alcohol.

Find yourself a good yeast supplier and work closely with that supplier. I currently source my yeast from White Labs (USA). I am impressed with their customer service and their Vodka, Whisky and Rum yeast strains all function well.

REFERENCES

Understanding Yeast Fundamentals, Inge Russell, Chapter 9, The Alcohol

Textbook, fourth edition, edited by Jacques, Lyons, Kelsall, Nottingham Press, U.K., 2003.

Enzymatic Conversion of Starch to Fermentable Sugars, Inge Russell, Chapter 9, The Alcohol Textbook, fourth edition, edited by Jacques, Lyons, Kelsall, Nottingham Press, U.K., 2003.

Fermented Beverage Production, first edition, edited by Andrew G.H. Lea, John R. Piggott, chapter 17, Flavor Chemistry, A. Paterson, J. Swanston, J. Piggot, Springer Press, 1995, USA.

Production of Aroma Compounds by Yeast, H. Suomaleinen and M. Lehtonen, Journal of the Institute of Brewing, May-June, vol 85, 1978.

Yeast, The Practical Guide to Beer Fermentation, Chris White & Jamil Zainasheff, Brewers Publications, USA, 2010.

6

WATER

Water is easily taken for granted. Distillers, however, should regard it for what it is – a critical raw material in the overall spirits production process.

What's In Your Water: The first step when it comes to water is to make a visit to a business in your community that retails water to the general public. These water sellers, such as Culligan, are required to have in their possession at any given time the most recent water quality analysis data for your community. Another way of obtaining water data is to talk to your local City Hall or visit their website to retrieve the water data.

When interpreting water quality data, there are some terms that you will encounter.

Hardness: this is a reference to the amount of Calcium and Magnesium in the water. Calcium and Magnesium are the constituents that contribute to hard scale build up on the showerheads and taps in your house.

Calcium ion (Ca^{2+}): Calcium ions are very important as they assist yeast in making invertase and protease enzymes. Calcium ions are also beneficial in helping the alpha and beta amylase enzymes in malted grain to perform optimally. Look for Calcium contents in the water analysis data to be 100 to 120 ppm. Lower amounts may require the addition of calcium to the mash water. Adding ¼ of a gram per liter of water will increase your Calcium content by 61 ppm. Calcium Sulfate (gypsum) powder is a suitable way to introduce extra Calcium to your water.

Magnesium (Mg^{2+}): Magnesium is also beneficial in the yeast growth cycle. The optimal amount of Magnesium in water is between 10 and 20 ppm. Adding a mere 1/8th of a gram to 1 Liter of water will raise the Magnesium level by 13 ppm.

Sodium (Na^{+}): 150 ppm is the most Sodium that can be tolerated by yeast. It is unlikely that Sodium levels in your water will ever be above 100 ppm. Sodium in small amounts will have a beneficial effect on flavors. In the rare cases where your water has extremely low levels of Sodium, consider adding minute amounts of Sodium Bicarbonate (Baking Soda). But, I must stress – minute amounts only.

Chloride (Cl^{-}): Chloride ions are not to be confused with atoms of Chlorine (Cl_2). Chlorides may be present in water in conjunction with Calcium. Chloride ions in water can help accentuate flavors. Most tap waters will have small, but adequate, amounts of Chloride ion present. Chlorine, on the other hand, is definitely toxic to yeast and must be avoided. If your tap water has the distinct aroma of Chlorine, be sure to pass the water through a basic 10 micron carbon block filter prior to using. Such filters are available from any water supply store.

Sulfate (SO_4^{2-}): Sulfates in water can lend a hand in promoting a crisp, clean taste. Beer brewers may seek out Sulfate in water. To a distiller, Sulfates are not that critical.

Nitrate (NO_3^{-}): Nitrates in water might come about if your community sources its water from an agricultural area where nearby farmers apply lots of Nitrate fertilizers. Nitrate ions are toxic to both yeast and humans.

Iron (Fe^{2+}, Fe^{3+}): Iron is toxic to yeast, so make sure your water is free of iron. This should not be an issue with tap water from your municipality, but if you are drawing well water, have it tested for iron.

Alkalinity ($CaCO_3$ or HCO^{3-}): Alkalinity is a very important constituent for it allows for the use of more acidic ingredients in the fermentation process. Think of those wonderful, heavy, Scottish Ales and Irish Stouts from areas of the world having high alkaline water. One distiller that is availing itself of local water with higher alkalinity is Corsair Distilling in Kentucky. They have come out with unique creations such as Oatmeal Stout Whisky, where the high alkalinity allows for the use of acidic, darker roasted and toasted grains. One area I have noted with a high alkaline content is the Okanagan Valley in British Columbia, Canada. The acidity of the grains added to mashes at Urban Distilleries is just enough to reduce the pH of the mash to 6.0. Were the alkalinity of the water any higher, the addition of small amounts of acid to the mash water would be essential. If in an area with high alkalinity, just remember that you are ideally seeking a mash pH of 5.5-5.8.

Total Dissolved Solids (TDS): when you have water that comes from your tap and it has a noticeable taste profile to it, it means there are tiny dissolved particles in the water. Collectively these tiny particles are termed Total Dissolved Solids. There is no guideline for how much TDS will or will not affect the outcome of a fermentation. My general approach is to pre-filter my water through a 10 micron carbon filter before using it in a fermentation. An excellent reference book to assist you with water chemistry is the previously mentioned *How to Brew* by author John Palmer. By way of nomograph charts, Palmer shows you how to adjust your water to deliver a desired Calcium or Bicarbonate level.

Geology will strongly influence the water chemistry in a particular area. For example, the city of Vancouver, Canada draws its drinking water from an area in the mountains north of the city. Water in Vancouver is practically devoid of mineral content. This is because granitic rock formations will impart few, if any, minerals to water. I have learned to avoid beer brewed in Vancouver for I find it severely lacking in body and taste profile. This is no doubt due to the lack of mineral content in the water which in turn has affected the fermentation process. Another area of Canada that has water with practically no mineral content is St. John's, Newfoundland which sits atop a massive geological deposit of granite.

Water from Dublin, Ireland has about 120 ppm Calcium and just over 300 ppm Alkalinity. The underlying limestone geology of the area is responsible. Water percolating through limestone rock formations will pick up mineral content. High water alkalinity levels in Dublin and surrounding area give brewers and distillers the latitude to add more acidic grains into the mash. Grains like roasted Barley, toasted Barley, chocolate malt and black patent malt are all acidic. The extra acidity is balanced by the alkalinity. This explains why the Irish for so many years have been enjoying success with the production of Guinness beer.

Localities such as Tennessee and Kentucky also sit atop massive limestone geological formations. Water in these areas also has higher alkalinity which affords the distiller the ability to use more acidic ingredients. And in fact this is what happens. The *sour mash* technique works very well in these parts and that has given birth to things like Tennessee Sour Mash Whisky. In the sour mash technique, some of the liquid added to the grist at the time of mashing is the acidic (low pH) spent *stillage* left over from a previous distillation run.

Water is further critical when it comes to proofing spirits. The details of proofing will be discussed in a later chapter. But, it is critical that spirits be proofed with top quality water so as to avoid imparting any off-flavors into the spirit. No customer wants to sip a Vodka and pick up notes of municipal tap water.

To provide this top quality water, one must source Reverse Osmosis water, otherwise known as R.O. water. A reverse osmosis machine comprises three parts. Incoming municipal water passes first through a filter bed to remove any heavy particulates. Next the filtered water passes through a water softener to remove Calcium ions. Lastly the softened water flow passes through a semi-permeable membrane made of material such as sodium acetate. The pore sizing on this membrane is such that the H_2O molecule will slip through but larger molecules will not. The result will be water that has a maximum impurity of only about 15 ppm total mineral content.

The diagram in Figure 9 illustrates a Reverse Osmosis flow. As a small batch distiller, you may not necessarily need a full blown Reverse Osmosis apparatus. There are many water vendors in large cities that will be all too happy to sell you bulk R.O. water.

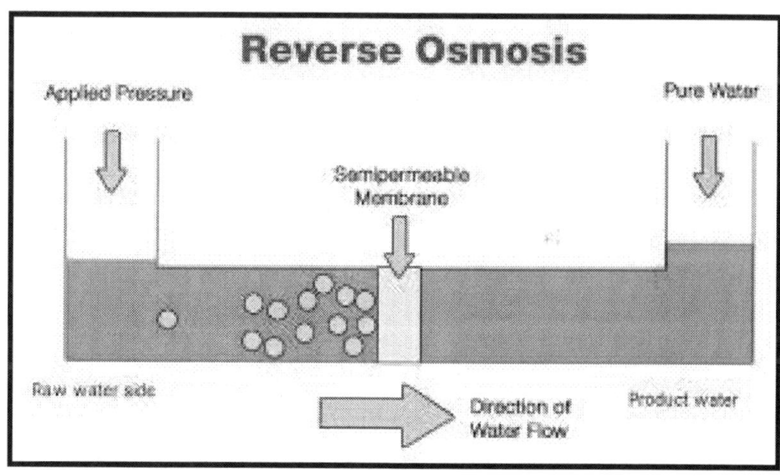

Figure 9 – Reverse Osmosis Process

REFERENCES

How to Brew, John Palmer, 2001, Defenstrative Publishing, USA.

Water, A Comprehensive Guide for Brewers, John Palmer and Colin Kaminski, Brewers Publications, USA.

7

DISTILLATION FUNDAMENTALS

The best way to understand distillation is to do it on a small still at home. As you do a distillation run, its concepts will quickly start to make intuitive sense to you. In this chapter, we will explore the basics of distillation.

BASIC CONCEPTS

There are several basic scientific concepts that must be explored as a lead-up to distillation.

Surface Tension: in nature, molecules will strive to exist in the state of lowest energy/greatest stability. With molecules in the liquid state, surface tension plays a role in helping to achieve this stability. For example, after you wash and wax your car, sprinkle some water on the freshly washed and waxed surface of your car. Notice that the water forms distinct, stable droplets. This is because the surface tension of the water droplets are greater than the forces of attraction between the water and the waxed surface of the car. As another example, add some water to a container of olive oil. Notice that the two liquids do not mix. The surface tension of the water is different than the surface tension of the oil and the oil will prefer to exist as stable droplets on the water surface.

Surface Tension and Boiling: consider a cup full of water (H_2O). The Oxygen atom in one molecule of water (water comprises 2 Hydrogens and 1 Oxygen) are attracted to the Hydrogen atoms in a nearby molecule of water. This attraction, called *hydrogen bonding,* is what provides water with its surface tension.

At the very surface of the cup of water, the water molecules are attracted to nothing – for above the surface is just air. This means that at the surface the water molecules have a net force pulling inwards towards the bulk of the water. This inward force is what prevents the water from escaping from the cup. The act of escaping from the cup is what we call *boiling*. Thus, liquids with a higher surface tension will have a higher boiling point than liquids with a lower surface tension.

As a numerical example, consider that water has a surface tension of 72 dynes/cm2 and a boiling point of 100C. Ethanol has a surface tension of 22.4 dynes/cm2 and a boiling point of 78.5C.

Mixtures and Boiling: consider a cup containing water. We know that the surface tension is 72 dynes/cm2 and the boiling point is 100C. Now, add some ethanol to this cup of water. We know that ethanol has a surface tension of 22.4 dynes/cm2 and a boiling point of 78.5C. The water molecules will be attracted to the ethanol molecule by way of hydrogen bonding. The resulting molecular configuration will have a surface tension that is somewhere between 72 and 22.4 dynes/cm^2 and a boiling point somewhere between 100 C and 78.5C. The exact surface tension and boiling point will be a function of the relative concentration of water and ethanol.

Vapor Pressure: take a small amount of liquid and place it in a closed container. Every liquid has a tendency to at least partly form some vapor. Vapor pressure is the pressure exerted by the vapor on the surrounding liquid inside our closed container. Vapor pressure is strictly a function of temperature and that function tends towards being an exponential relationship. There are several ways of expressing vapor pressure. I typically prefer the old fashioned non-metric units of millimeters of Mercury (mmHg). For example, water at 30C has a vapor pressure of 33.3 mm Hg. Water at a temperature of 50C will have a vapor pressure of 92.5 mm Hg. (Another unit of measure you may encounter when dealing with vapor pressure is the

Torr. Units of Torr and mm Hg are pretty much the same thing). The atmosphere around us exerts a downward pressure on us of 760 mm Hg. In order for a liquid to boil, it must have a vapor pressure that equals or exceeds 760 mm Hg.

If vapor pressure is a function of temperature, this then implies that if we heat a liquid and impart energy to it, we can raise its vapor pressure. Imparting enough heat energy to make the vapor pressure equal to 760 mm Hg will result in that liquid breaking its surface tension at the surface of a container.

In other words, imparting sufficient heat energy to a liquid will make it *boil.* If a liquid has a fairly high vapor pressure at room temperature to begin with, it will take relatively less added heat energy to eventually raise the vapor pressure to 760 mm Hg. Ethanol has a vapor pressure at 30C of 65 mm Hg. Water has a vapor pressure at 30C of 33.3 mm Hg. This means then that ethanol will require less added heat energy than water to arrive at 760 mm Hg and boiling. This is why we say that ethanol has a lower boiling temperature (78.5 C) than water (100C).

Raoult's Law: Francois Raoult was a French physicist who lived in the mid-1800s. He devoted his scientific studies to understanding the behavior of liquid-liquid systems. One such system he studied was the water-ethanol system. The culmination of Raoult's work, *Raoult's Law,* states that the vapor pressure of a liquid-liquid system such as water-ethanol is equal to the respective amounts of water and alcohol in the mixture.

$$P(total) = (x1*P1) + (x2*P2) ;$$

where x1 and x2 are the mole fractions of water and ethanol respectively, P1 is the vapor pressure of water alone and P2 is the vapor pressure of ethanol alone.

This equation shows that as the amount of ethanol in a water/ethanol solution increases, the vapor pressure will likewise increase. Therefore, as the amount of ethanol in the solution increases, the boiling point decreases. Through repeated and careful study, Raoult came to understand this relationship in intimate detail and constructed a visual representation which is illustrated in Figure 10.

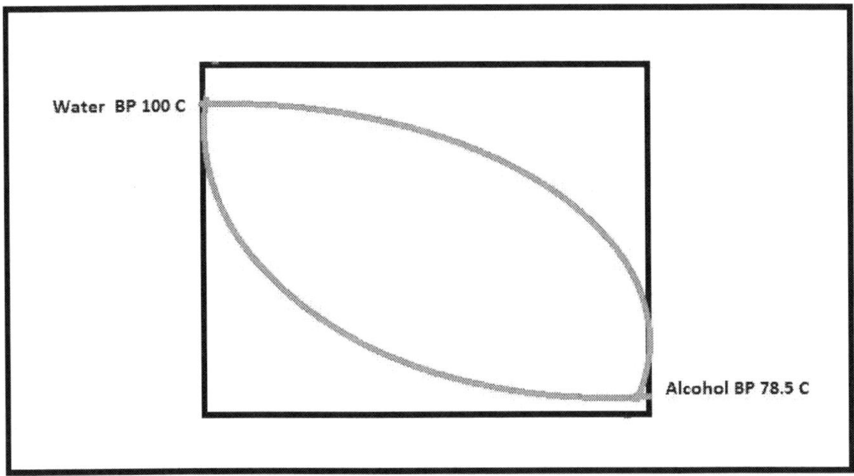

Figure 10 A Visual Representation of Raoult's Law

Hydrogen Bonding: any molecule with a H (Hydrogen) atom or an O (Oxygen) atom as part of its makeup is capable of electrostatically attaching to another molecule with an H or an O atom. This is the aforementioned *hydrogen bonding.*

As has been discussed, the fermentation process generates a family of alcohols. In fact, the myriad of products resulting from a ferment includes alcohols such as propanol, butanol, n-methyl-n-propanol, n-methyl-n-butanol, isoamyl alcohol, iso-amyl acetate to name but a few. Even yeast synthesizing fatty acids can create alcohols. These various alcohols are all capable of being attracted to one another.

A good analogy for hydrogen bonding is that of two friends. One day they may hang out together, the next day they may not. The degree of hydrogen bonding is temperature dependent. As temperature rises, more Hydrogen bonding can occur. The point of this discussion then is that during distillation, an ethanol molecule may emerge from the still with a few passengers attached. Then again, it may emerge from the still with plenty of baggage attached. Technical literature says that alcohols with 1,2,3 and maybe 4 Carbon atoms are capable of exhibiting hydrogen bonding.

Depending on how and where a Hydrogen or Oxygen atom attaches itself to another molecule will determine the nature of that molecule. For example, propanol will have an Oxygen atom attached in a different location than iso-propanol. Each of these molecules created by Hydrogen Bonding will have its own unique vapor pressure and boiling point. In many cases, the boiling points of these molecules will be in close proximity to that of ethanol (78.5C).

Molecules at Boiling: during distillation, when sufficient heat energy has been imparted to any one of these alcohol family molecules, consider what happens. Does propanol by itself turn to vapor? Does ethanol by itself turn to vapor? In fact, what happens is very complex and it relates back to the ideas of surface tension and hydrogen bonding. With sufficient heat energy imparted, ethanol will achieve its boiling point. But, the surface tension of the ethanol molecules and the surface tension of any other molecules present mean that some of these other molecules could be taken along for a ride, so to speak, as the ethanol boils. The same scenario applies to all the other alcohol family molecules as they attain their various boiling points.

Purification: consider a container containing watery liquid from a fermentation along with various molecular members of the alcohol family. Heat that container to 95C and vapors will rise from the container. Those vapors will comprise ethanol plus various other alcohol family members plus some attached water and/or other molecules. Capture the vapors and cool them down. Now drink the resulting liquid. Yes indeed – it will impart that feeling of pleasure that early mankind recognized as intoxication. Will this liquid be utterly delicious and full of layers of flavor? No, it will not. But it will be passable as an alcoholic beverage.

Circle back now to Raoult's Law which states that as the amount of higher vapor pressure component in a solution increases, the boiling point of the solution decreases slightly. Take the captured alcoholic liquid in this example and heat it again. This time it will boil at something perhaps approaching 90 C. Capture the vapors and cool them down. Now taste the liquid. It will be somewhat better than the previous iteration and will comprise more ethanol and slightly fewer other molecules because the heat energy has caused the ethanol to break free of its passengers.

Take this liquid and heat it again. Raoult's Law tells us that because it has a higher concentration of higher vapor pressure molecules, it will have a lower boiling point. This time it may boil at something closer to 82C. Capture the vapor and cool it. It will taste smoother than the previous iterations. It will contain fewer water molecules, fewer other alcohol family members and quite a lot of ethanol molecules. The heat energy imparted to make it boil was sufficient to break the surface tension between the various molecules. Because the concentration of ethanol molecules has been increased by this latest boiling effort, the vapor pressure of the overall solution is increased.

Heat it again and this time it may boil at something near 80C. The taste will be further improved. Heat it again and this time you will find it boils at 78.5C and the resulting captured liquid will have a very desirable taste sensation on the tongue – for it will consist of mostly ethanol. This rather convoluted story describes how alcoholic liquid present after a fermentation can be purified by successive vaporizing and cooling iterations.

Azeotrope: Raoult understood this process intimately and was able to graphically describe it using a diagram similar to what appears in Figure 11.

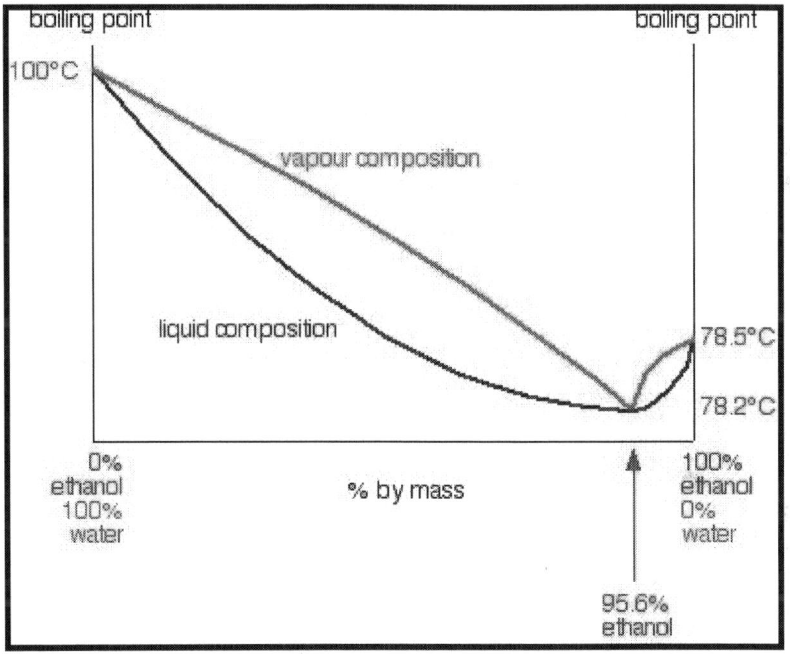

Figure 11 Azeotropic Point in the Ethanol-Water System

Note that at the right side of the curve there is a small tail of sorts. Using repeated vaporizations and condensations, there is a limit to how pure one can make the an ethanol/water solution. Raoult determined that the maximum vapor pressure in the water-ethanol system occurred at 78.2 C and an ethanol concentration of 95.6 %. This is called the *azeotropic point* and this is the purest that a distiller will ever get when producing ethanol. But, ethanol does not have to be at its azeotropic point to be drinkable and enjoyable. This means one does not necessarily need to invest in ultra-expensive distilling equipment. I know of several home distillers who are making product that contains 92 % ethanol which is perfectly drinkable. I have tasted craft distilled Vodka made on small stills that is very good also. In a coming chapter on Distillery Equipment we will explore various equipment options available to the small batch distiller.

Heat Energy: Take a pot of water and place it on your stovetop. Turn the heat on and bring the water to a boil. How quickly did it manage to attain a boil? Repeat this exercise with a much larger pot full of water. How quickly did it attain boiling? There is relationship to energy required and mass that is expressed:

$$Q=m*Cp*(\text{delta } T) ;$$

where m is the mass of liquid being heated, Cp is the specific heat capacity of the liquid being heated and delta T is the temperature range through which you are heating the liquid.

The point here is that as a small batch distiller, you must be cognizant that the larger your still, the more heat energy you will require. If running a still heated by steam, this will entail a larger steam boiler for larger volume stills. If heating your still by means of an immersed electrical heating element, the larger the still, the more heating elements that will be needed. Keep this in mind as you begin sourcing equipment.

Latent Heats: continuing on with our example of a pot on a stovetop, notice what happens when that pot starts to boil. Does all of the water in the pot instantly turn to vapor and rush out of the pot? No, it does not. It takes time and plenty of heat energy to move the mass of water from its liquid state to a gaseous (vapor) state. This is the concept of *Latent Heat of Vaporization* (LHV).

Consider now some steam vapor. Expose that vapor to a tube through which is flowing cold water. Does all the steam contacting the cold tube immediately turn to a liquid? No it does not. There is a considerable amount of energy that must be given up in order to condense the steam vapor. This is the concept of *Latent Heat of Condensation* (LHC).

POTS & COLUMNS

A Pot Still: Consider the schematic of a simple pot still as illustrated in Figure 12.

Consider what happens when this still is filled with liquid from a fermentation vessel. That liquid will contain water plus the various alcohol family members.

Consider what happens as heat energy is applied to the underside of the still. At a temperature approaching perhaps 58C°, the acetone (C_3H_6O) molecule with some water molecules attached to it by way of hydrogen bonding will break the surface tension of the liquid and will rise up the still. As the vapors hit the cooler upper reaches of the still, the vapors will lose heat energy into the Copper metal of the still and will return to a liquid form, dribbling down the interior surface of the still.

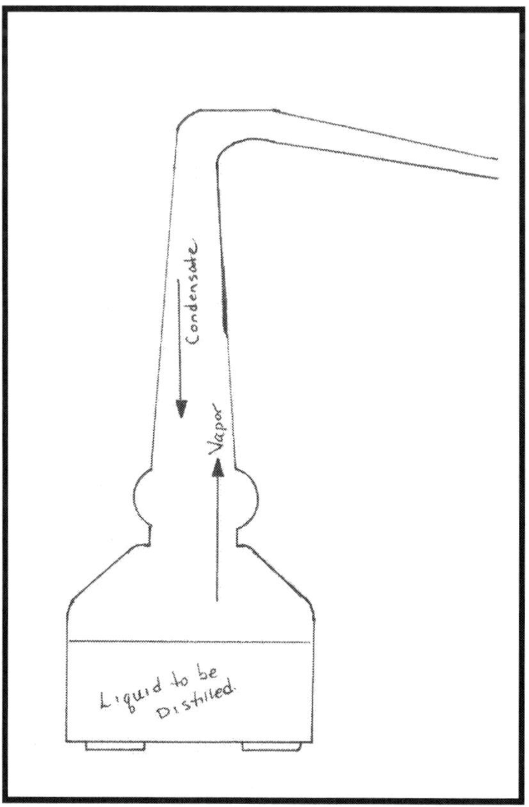

Figure 12 Schematic of a Copper Pot Still

But dribble far, they will not. For as soon as the liquid picks up more heat energy, the liquid will return to vapor form. This condensation and vaporization will break most of the hydrogen bonds that attract the water molecules and in accordance with Raoult's Law, the boiling point will now be nearer to perhaps 56C which is the boiling point of pure acetone. With some repeated vaporizations and condensations, the Copper metal in the still heats up further. With the still being warmer, the vapors will be able to rise up to the top of the still and find their way down the goose neck shaped *lyne arm* and into the condenser.

But, the process is not complete. Heat energy is continually being applied to the pot still which is getting warmer. The next molecule to attain enough energy to break the surface tension will be methanol and it will have water and perhaps other molecules in tow. The methanol molecule with other molecules attached will rise up through the still. Somewhere near the top of the pot, these vapors will condense and begin to dribble back down the interior surface of the still. As soon as sufficient heat energy is regained, these methanol molecules will turn to vapor again. In accordance with Raoult's Law, the newly re-vaporized molecules will have fewer other molecules attached and will have a lower boiling point. As the vapors rise again, they lose heat energy which is imparted to the Copper pot causing it to heat up marginally further. This loss of heat energy causes condensation and the methanol molecules dribble down the inside of the pot. But, they have been further purified and with a marginally lower boiling point they soon re-vaporize and start rising. This time they make it to the top of the pot and enter the lyne arm and travel to the condenser. These lower boiling point molecules (aldehydes, acetones and methanols) are what distillers term the *Heads*.

The next molecule to consider is ethanol. As was discussed in the chapter on fermentation, ethanol will comprise the majority of the alcohol molecules present after a fermentation. The pot still continues to be gently heated. The heat energy being imparted to the pot is now being taken up by the ethanol molecules. This is the above noted concept of Latent Heat of Vaporization at work. It takes a fair amount of heat energy to ultimately cause such a relatively large mass of ethanol to change from liquid to vapor phase. Once sufficient heat energy has been absorbed by the ethanol, it will strive to break the surface tension and with some water molecules (and other alcohols) in tow, ethanol molecules will start rising up the pot still. When these molecules run out of sufficient heat energy to remain in vapor phase, they condense and begin to dribble down the interior walls of the still. These molecules quickly regain heat energy and vaporize again.

In compliance with Raoult's Law, they are now further purified and have a lower boiling point. As they rise up through the pot still, they rise further before condensing. After several successive iterations, the ethanol molecules enter the lyne arm and journey onwards to the condenser. This is what a distiller calls the *Hearts*.

Heat energy continues to be applied to the pot still. Next in succession to break the surface tension and start boiling will be the various higher molecular weight members of the alcohol family all with boiling points slightly above that of ethanol. These family members will eventually make it to the top of the pot still and enter the lyne arm. This is what a distiller calls the *Tails*.

Here is where the art of distillation enters the picture. With a pot still, the number of iterations of vaporizing and condensing is somewhat limited by the surface area of the pot. The ethanol collected by the distiller will have other alcohol molecules attached. In addition, in a distillation, the distiller has to decide when and where to stop collecting Tails distillate. Collect too much Tails material and the distillate will contain too many of the heavier molecules such as propanol, butanol and the like. This will mean a distillate that has a notable harsh burn on the tongue. Such distillate will also deliver a notable headache and hangover the next morning to the imbibing consumer. In the corporate world of mass produced alcoholic spirits, the presence of too many Tails in the distillate is why many cheaper brands of Whisky have a notable burn on the palate. This is why consumers have learned to mix these cheaper brands of spirits with soda pop – to cover up the burn.

Why then, you ask, do the Scots continue to make their malt Whisky using pot stills and why is much of their Whisky so tasty? True enough – the product of a pot distillation process will not be ultra-smooth by any stretch of the imagination. The answer rests with the fact that when these denser alcohol molecules are allowed to mellow in an oak cask, they oxidize over time and the oxidized products actually create more flavorful molecules, especially when combined with the organic acids from the oak wood. But, more on this in a future chapter.

Anneas Coffey: in the mid-1800s, the head of Excise Collections for the Irish Government was a gentleman by the name of Anneas Coffey. He was a clever man by many accounts and he decided that there had to be a more efficient way to distill Whisky than with a pot still. What he ended up devising is illustrated in Figure 13.

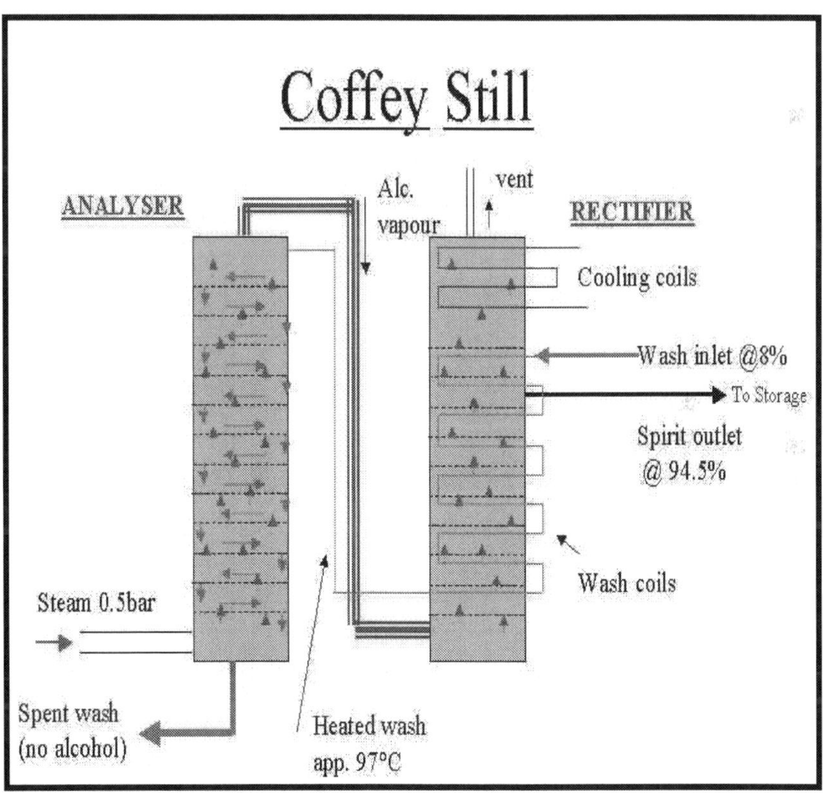

Figure 13 Coffey Still

The secret to his Coffey Still (sometimes called the Patent Still) is the horizontal plates at regular intervals up the column. This invention is what paved the way for the modern column stills that you may have seen in craft distilleries.

The Column Still: different still makers will utilize different design configurations for their plates ranging from small bubble caps to inverted domes to perforated sieve plates. The diagram in Figure 14 illustrates a simplified series of plates in a column still.

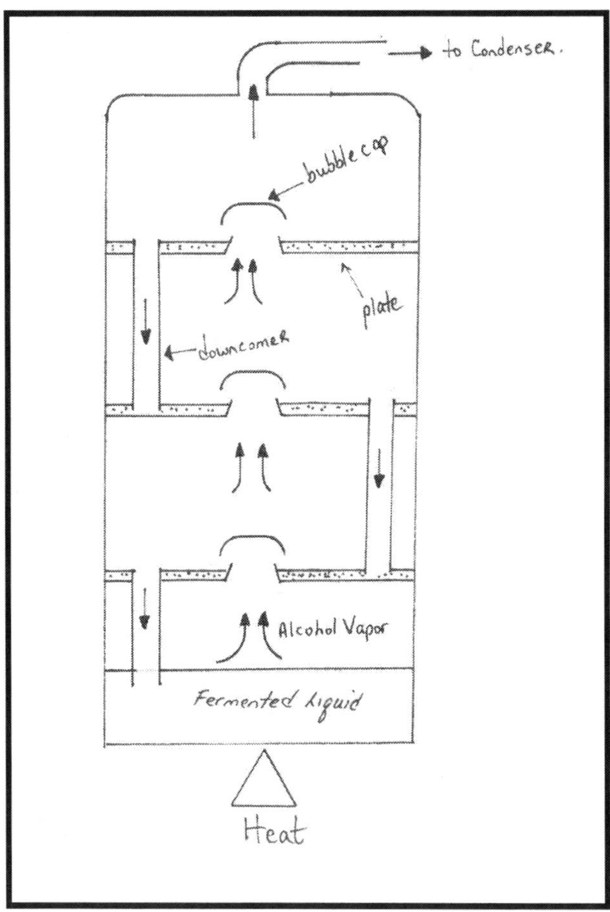

Figure 14 Simplified Schematic of Plates in a Column Still

Prior to commencing a distillation run, the distiller will turn on the internal cleaning system in the column and allow a small amount of water to be collected at each plate. When the distillation run starts, heat energy will be applied to the pot containing the liquid from the fermentation tank.

As with the previous example of a simple pot still, the first molecule to attain sufficient heat energy to break the surface tension in the pot will be acetone and it will have water molecules attached to it. The acetone and its passengers will rise from the pot and enter the column. Heat energy will be absorbed by the mass of Copper in the column and the acetone molecule will condense and dribble back down towards the pot. Raoult's Law is still very much in force here and this act of vaporization and condensation will cause the acetone to become purified and take on a lower boiling point.

Through subsequent repeated vaporizations and condensations, the acetone molecules will make the journey to the top of the column and onwards to the condenser. The next molecule to break the surface tension will be methanol. These first members to exit the distillation are called Heads, just as in the previous discussion of a pot still. The repeated vaporizations and condensations have imparted heat to the column still, similar to how the pot still was heated in the previous example.

Next up are the ethanol molecules. The concept here is the same as in the previous discussion on what happens to ethanol in the pot still. The major difference, however, between the pot still and the column still is internal surface area. The column still with its plates, bubble caps and associated hardware has more surface area and hence more opportunities for molecules to repeatedly vaporize and condense. As molecules condense, they dribble downwards only to collect in the water layer present on the plates. As the molecules regain heat energy, they rise from the plate and travel upwards, purified in accordance with Raoult's Law.

With a column still, the right side of Raoult's curve comes into play. With sufficient plates, column height and internal surface area, clean alcoholic distillates can be generated with ethanol content at or approaching the azeotropic point of 96.5 % ethanol.

If you are a connoisseur of good quality Vodka, you will quickly be able to spot the quality differences between craft distillers who are using a tall column with as many as 14 plates and those who are using a short column with fewer than six plates. Three examples of truly outstanding Vodka in Canada come from Urban Distilleries in Kelowna, BC, Park Distilling in Banff, Alberta and Black Fox Spirits in Saskatoon, Saskatchewan. Each of these distilleries employs large German-made column stills.

For a start-up craft distiller who does not have a large capital budget for the purchase of one of these beautiful German-made stills, it is possible to re-distill the distillate obtained from a distillation run on a still with six plates to bring about further purification. In 2015, while visiting Hillbilly Stills in Barlow, Kentucky I was offered a sample of Lost Soldier Vodka from Soldier Valley Spirits in Nebraska that was running a 150 gallon Hillbilly still with an 8 inch diameter column and 6 plates. By conducting a few successive distillation runs, the distiller was able to produce a clean, delicious Vodka that I quite enjoyed sipping. In my experience, a six plate column is the minimum that a craft distiller should consider when sourcing a still.

REFERENCES:

The Compleat Distiller, Nixon & McCaw, Amphora Society, USA, 2010

The Alcohol Textbook, fourth edition, chapter 17, From Pot Stills to Continuous Stills, R. Piggot, Nottingham University Press, U.K., 2003.

8

DISTILLERY EQUIPMENT

With an examination of raw materials, water, yeast, fermentation and distillation now behind us, the question arises – what does one need for equipment to start making alcoholic spirits? What follows is an explanation of equipment needed for both a home distiller making small batches for personal consumption only and a craft distiller seeking to make small batch product for licensed, legal sale to the public.

Processing Mill: raw materials have to be crushed or otherwise ground prior to starting a mash. Home distillers using grain as a raw material will want to obtain a hand-cranked roller mill. These are readily obtainable from home brewing stores and websites specializing in home brewing equipment. Home distillers using fruit or grape as a raw material will want to get a fruit press or durable food processor. Many home wine-making shops will rent fruit presses. Craft distillers will want to obtain a larger format roller mill or a hammer mill if using grains as raw material. For fruit and grape material, most makers of high capacity mash pumps also will sell a hopper attachment for the mash pump that will allow you to add fruit to the hopper. The fruit will be crushed and ground as it passes through the auger of the mash pump. There are also machines that tumble fruit and cause the flesh to be scraped from the pits. Most of these will be typically sourced from Italy.

Mash Vessel: when working with grains they have to be cooked as outlined in the chapter called Raw Materials. Home distillers have many cheap and easy selections at hand. Any website dedicated to home beer making will have brew kettles for sale. Sizes will range from 10 liter all the way up to 120 liter. Construction will be stainless steel. Some of the cheaper models will be made from Chinese 200 grade stainless which will over time blemish and stain. If top quality is your desire and if you have the budget, choose brew kettles from Blichmann Engineering which will most assuredly be made from 304 grade stainless and will last you a lifetime.

Craft distillers will be faced with a wide selection of stainless mash tanks, all with different features. Sizes will range from as small as 600 liters to as large as 1800 liters. When considering mash tanks, decide how you wish to heat your grain mash. It is possible to source tanks with a steam port in them that will allow you to inject steam direct from a steam boiler into the mash. It is also possible to source tanks that have a steam jacket built into the bottom 1/3 of the tank. Steam will circulate through this jacketed portion and never physically contact the grain mash. I have seen both types in operation and in all cases the distillers swore by their choice of mash tank design. It is probably wise to travel around to different craft distilleries and speak to distillers before making a purchase.

The cooling capacity of the mash tank is another matter to consider. As discussed in the chapter called Yeast & Fermentation, different yeast suppliers will offer products that are designed to perform at different temperatures. In the case of Lallemand yeast, it is engineered to function optimally at 30C. This means that after you have completed the mash, you should cool the mash to 30C, pump it over to your fermentation tank, add your yeast, and then have a cooling system on the fermentation tank ensure the heat generated by fermentation does not cause the mash temperature to rise above 30C. Such a cooling system will entail a refrigerated glycol system with the glycol tubes wrapped around the circumference of the mash vessel.

A glycol cooling system big enough to service both a mash tank plus fermentation tanks will mean a significant added cost to your startup budget. In the case of White Labs yeast, it is engineered to perform at temperatures in the 22-25C range. So, one could potentially cool the mash tank down with the glycol cooling unit to under 25C, pump it to the fermenter tank and add the yeast. The ferment will be exothermic and will generate heat, but water flowing through the cooling jackets on the fermenter tank on as as-needed basis would probably suffice.

When working with fruits, grapes or molasses, a modest amount of heat input will be required. Fruits and grapes contain a protein called *pectin*. During fermentation, yeast can react with pectin to form a methyl pectate, a close relative of methanol which is an undesirable compound in any distilled spirit beverage.

One technique for limiting the amount of methyl pectate is to heat the mash of fruit or grapes to near 40C and hold that temperature for 30 minutes. The yeast can be added when the temperature has subsided back down to something at or less than 30C depending on the strain of yeast being utilized. I have personally used this approach and can attest that the amount of Heads material generated during the distillation run is no more than would be generated from a typical distillation of a wash made from fermenting grain.

As for molasses, it is advisable to heat the mixture of molasses and water (plus any added sugar) to 40-50C to thoroughly dissolve the molasses and sugars.

Fermentation Vessel: home distillers have many options available to them for fermentation vessels. For the past 30 years I personally have never strayed too far from food-grade plastic fermentation pails purchased from a local home brewing store.

If your budget permits, you can purchase stainless steel fermenter vessels from on-line vendors. The quality of these vessels will vary according to place of origin. As noted in the previous section, if you want top of the line equipment, Blichmann Engineering is the place to go. Craft distillers too have many options. There are vendors of stainless steel fermenter tanks in Canada, the USA, Germany, Croatia and just about everywhere in between. One Canadian form that is gaining a reputation for providing tanks to the craft distilling industry is Ripley Stainless from Summerland, British Columbia. Another that is emerging is Stewart Steel from Weyburn, Saskatchewan.

The issue of cooling is important. As noted previously, Lallemand yeasts are engineered to function at 30C. If pitching the yeast and commencing fermentation at 30C, cooling fluid must be allowed to circulate around the entire circumference of the tank to avoid temperature rising above 30C and damaging the yeast. With other yeast suppliers, it will be possible to commence the fermentation at a lower temperature. In cases like this, cooling capability on only a portion of the tank circumference will suffice.

I have seen many configurations of fermentation tanks being used in the craft distilleries I have visited. It is probably wise to travel to various craft distilleries and talk to the owners. Do your due diligence before making a purchasing decision.

Pumps and Hoses: for home distillers, pumps and hoses is a non-issue. You will be making mashes in small quantity and using pumps to move material will not be required. Craft distillers, however, will be in need of a mash pump and associated hoses as larger volumes of material will be handled.

There are many manufacturers of mash pumps. Most will be European based, although with some searching you will also find North American manufacturers. If sourcing from outside North America and if electrical inspection is a concern, make sure the pump motors are certified for both 50Hz and 60Hz. A good way of finding mash pump vendors is to speak to any company that currently supplies equipment to the beer or wine industry. There are many vendors of hoses on the marketplace. Be sure that you are buying hose that is food grade quality and if planning to pump hot mash or hot liquids, be sure the hose in question is temperature rated.

Heat Source: for home distillers, the most efficient source of heat for heating the contents of the mash vessel will be a propane cylinder and associated burner. You will easily find these burners at any of the big-name hardware stores. Many people use these burners in their back-yards for deep-frying turkeys and other foods.

Craft distillers are faced with a bit more complexity when it comes to heat sources. A steam boiler will be the heat source needed. Every province in Canada and every state in America will have its own unique rules and regulations governing steam boilers. Some jurisdictions will state that if the boiler output rating is above a certain threshold, then a certified, steam-ticketed boiler technician will be required to do the installation and to make any subsequent operational adjustments. This can quickly become an expensive proposition. Other jurisdictions will simply say that so long as the boiler is a low pressure unit, any local plumbing and heating contractor can assist you with the install and maintenance. Before talking to any boiler provider, do your homework and check the wording of your local legislation concerning boilers. With the legislation understood, the next discussion to be had will be with the manufacturer of your still. Every still maker will know the amount of heat energy required to most efficiently run their design of still. Heat energy requirements may be expressed as British Thermal Units (BTU/hour) or as Horsepower (H.P.) or as Pounds of Steam per Hour.

One Boiler Horsepower is equal to 33,475 BTU/Hr.

Boiler Horsepower x 34.5 = Pounds of Steam per Hour.

If the boiler threshold in your jurisdiction happens to be restrictive, it is possible to run boilers in tandem. For example, the Canadian province of British Columbia has a threshold of 400,000 BTU. A craft distiller needing, say, 800,000 BTU of capacity would be better off installing two units at 400,000 BTU each than having to deal with expensive steam-ticketed technicians for installation and maintenance.

Still: for home distillers, there are an ever-increasing number of options. I know of two vendors in Portugal for sourcing small Copper alembic stills. One type of Copper still is the classic *bain-marie* style which is essentially a double boiler. The liquid to be distilled is held in a pot which in turn is surrounded by a larger pot containing water. As the still is heated, it is the outer water bath that uniformly heats the inner pot of alcoholic liquid.

Figure 15 Bain Marie Still

The other type of Copper still you will find in Portugal is the standard alembic still with no water jacketing. Care must be taken not add too many solids to the pot for fear that the solids scorch during distillation and impart burnt flavors to your distillate.

Figure 16 Alembic Still for Home Use

Home distillers I have talked to claim they have never had any difficulties ordering from these Portuguese suppliers. They place their orders on-line and within two weeks their stills arrived via Fed-Ex or UPS.

To take your home distilling to the next level, one should seriously consider a pot and a column type of still design. There are a handful of vendors who offer these stills. I have a personal preference for Hillbilly Stills from Barlow, Kentucky. My travels have taken me to visit their manufacturing facility in Kentucky where I had a chance to witness up close and personal their team of craftsman working on the components that comprise a typical Hillbilly Still.

A Hillbilly Still consists of a stainless steel pot that utilizes a 5500 watt heating element. This is the same element that is in a typical residential electric hot water heater. The heating element draws its power from a standard residential 220 Volt outlet and a 30 Amp breaker. If you are worried your house may not have such an outlet, don't be. Your clothes dryer receptacle is a 220 Volt, 30 Amp service. The stainless steel pot of a Hillbilly Still is available in 13 US gallon and 28 US gallon sizes. The copper columns atop the stainless steel pot come in two configurations – 4 plate and 6 plate. The 4 plate is ideal for making Whisky distillate. The 6 plate is ideally suited for making a Vodka distillate with 92 % alcohol. Figure 17 illustrates a typical Hillbilly Still.

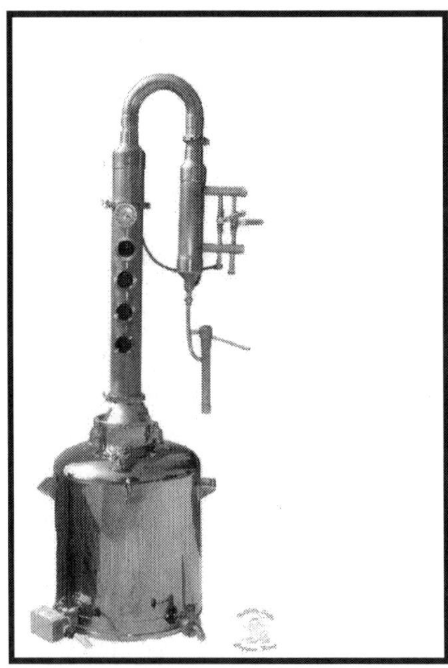

Figure 17 Hillbilly Still for Home Distillation

Decide on what features you want before rushing into a buying decision. Talk to other home distillers on the various on-line chat rooms. Do your homework. The still you ultimately buy will be with you for many years to come.

Craft distillers face an ever-increasing number of options when it comes to stills. The major factor at play will be your capital budget. There are German still makers that have been in business for 100+ years such as Kothe, Holstein, Carl, and Mueller. These brand names will command above average prices. Demand for these popular names has become so intense that it now will take up to 24 months for delivery once you have placed your order and made payment.

This market tightness has resulted in other companies moving in to fill the supply gap. Hillbilly Stills has now launched a sister-company HBS Coppers that makes Copper pots up to 175 US gallons (660 liters) in size. Distillation columns of 6, 8 or 10 inches are available with plate configurations of between 6 and 12. I have seen one of these stills in operation at the Moonshine Company in Paducah, Kentucky and was very impressed with the quality of the distillate being produced.

Another American firm that entered the playing field in 2012 is Corson Distilling from Idaho. I personally have not seen their stills, but a recent Workshop attendee has ordered one for his craft distillery in Park City, Utah.

An Italian still-maker called Barison is also active in the North American market now through its representative Prospero Ltd. I have seen these Italian stills and tasted the product created on them. I am suitably impressed.

There are even North American firms having stills made in China for distribution to craft distillers starting up in Canada and America. I have heard widely mixed reviews on these products and on other stills made in China. Two firms in particular that are sourcing stills from China are Confederated Stills of Alabama and Artisan Stills. Based on the information provided to me by craft distillers using these Chinese built products, my advice is to travel around and visit craft distilleries. Speak with the distillers, taste their products and decide wisely. Be very cautious if approached by a vendor selling stainless steel column stills. A fermentation will generate sulfur compounds in trace amounts. If left unchecked, these compounds will travel through the distillation process to leave a slight burning sensation in the distillate. The only way to remove sulfur compounds is by way of copper. A distillation column made of copper will react with the sulfurs to produce a copper-sulfate which adheres to the inner wall of the column and does not end up in the final distillate.

A final note on the subject of stills pertains to Gin. The botanicals added to make Gin contain essential oils. These oils have a nasty habit of adhering to still internal surfaces, gaskets and piping joints. If making Gin, it might be advisable to purchase a small, dedicated still that you will use for Gin alone. This will save you the tedium of having to scrub your still clean before using it for a distillation run of something other than Gin.

Filtration: craft distillers making a Vodka will want to filter the product before selling it to the consumer. Some craft distillers are even filtering their Whisky distillates through various types of wood charcoal.

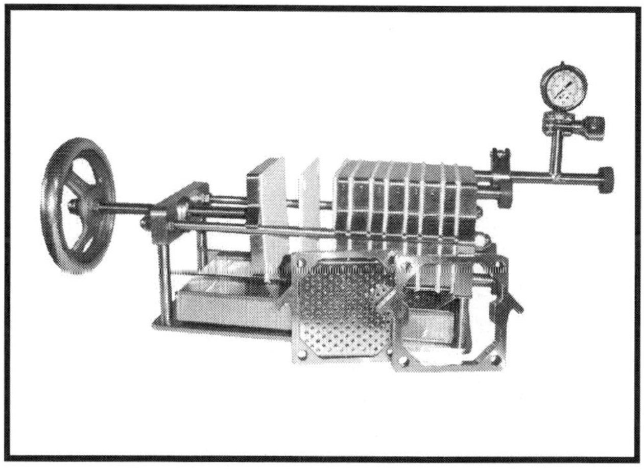

Figure 18 Plate and Frame filter

There are plate and frame type filtration systems available as well as cartridge type systems as illustrated in Figures 18 and 19.

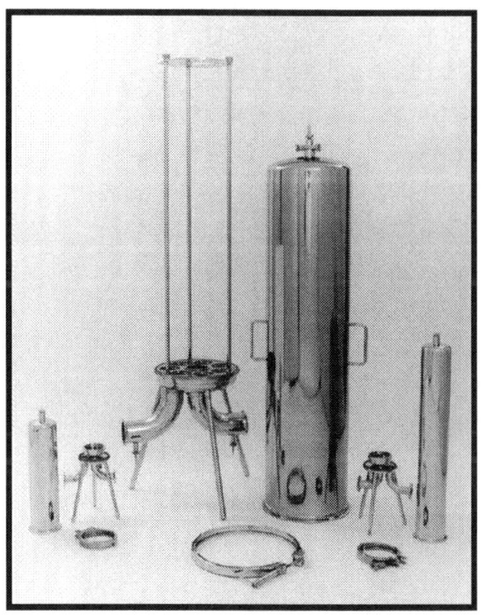

Figure 19 Cartridge filter

Plate and frame filters accommodate square filter pads with pore spacings of as fine as 0.5 microns. When using a plate and frame filter, the alcohol distillate is first mixed with charcoal. The distillate is then pumped through the plate and frame filter where the filter pads remove any trace amounts of charcoal.

Cartridge filter systems accommodate Carbon cartridges with a variety of pore sizes available. There are a number of filtration vendors in the marketplace. Do your homework and talk to other craft distillers to see what they are using.

Blending Tanks: a craft distiller will need one or more blending tanks where alcoholic distillate can be diluted (proofed) with water to reduce the strength to the desired level for sale to the customer. There are no shortage of vendors in the marketplace who can provide small, stainless steel blending tanks of size 300 to 600 liters.

Bottle Filling: there are a number of makers of bottle filling devices in the marketplace. You will be limited only by your imagination and your budget. The most common design you will find will be the level filler type. You configure the fill nozzles so that each bottle gets filled to the same level. The liquid will flow into each bottle by gravity. An economical design for small craft distillers will be one that holds four bottles at a time. Bottles will be placed on the filler and removed by hand once filled.

Closures: there are two options available for bottle closures – corks and screw caps. Natural corks are becoming something of a contentious issue thanks to global warming which has resulted in organic compounds now being present in natural cork. Cork, by the way, is the thick bark that grows on the Portuguese oak tree. If the alcoholic liquid in a bottle comes in contact with a natural cork closure there is a risk that these organic compounds may leach from the cork. The result can be off-color and off-taste developing in the alcoholic beverage. This is why the closure industry has now developed synthetic cork materials. It is strongly advised that synthetic cork closures be sourced if you don't want customers complaining about your product quality. If a cork closure is not what a craft distiller wants in terms of brand image, there are any number of screw cap products available in the marketplace. A capping machine will be necessary to install these types of closures. Shop around and consider different vendors. The cost of a capping machine could be significant.

Bottles: there was a time when North America boasted bottle manufacturing facilities. Sadly, many of these have closed – unable to compete with the cheaper products coming from China. If sourcing bottles from China, bear in mind that while the overall quality might be decent, it is reasonable to expect some variations in the tolerance of the bottle opening. If using cork as a closure, expect, some corks to fit tight and others to fit not so tight. To avoid this sloppy tolerance issue, it is advisable to source bottles from a European manufacturer. Take a look at the bottles of spirits for sale at a typical liquor store. Pick up some bottles. Feel them. In your mind, how do you judge a heavier bottle versus a lighter bottle? Studies have suggested that a consumer will regard the spirit in a heavier bottle as having greater quality. Look at the shapes of bottles. Are there some shapes that are easier to grasp than others? The bottle you ultimately choose for your craft distilled product will be what gives a potential customer his or her first impression of your product. Choose carefully. Be somewhat wary too of custom molded bottles. For the cost of several thousand dollars, one can engage a Chinese glass maker to prepare you a custom designed bottle. Be very certain that there are no hidden restrictions on minimum order sizes of custom bottles. Be certain too that the supplier in China will be able to deliver according to your needs. I have heard of craft distillers getting hit with large, expensive minimum order quantities. I recently heard of a craft distiller who placed an order for custom made bottles and then proceeded to launch a marketing campaign for the release of its Whisky. As the release date neared, the Chinese supplier called to advise that they were not happy with how the custom molds had turned out and that it would be several more months before the bottles would arrive in Canada.

Labels: take a stroll through your local liquor store. Look at the various bottles of product for sale. Notice that many spirit makers are using labels that are adhesively applied. A good number of other producers are using bottles that have information screened onto the bottle. Which method makes the strongest impression on you? Are there certain colors that you feel more attracted to? Studies have shown that green is suggestive of nature, balance and harmony. Red is suggestive of heat, power and action. Yellow is suggestive of happiness and cheerfulness. Yellow is also an attention-getter, which is why many taxi cabs are yellow. One excellent use of yellow can be seen with a Canadian product called *Ungava Gin*. The makers of this Gin have taken the unprecedented step of coloring their Gin yellow which makes it practically jump off the shelf when placed beside other Gin brands that are colorless. The color Gold suggests richness and extravagance. The same can be said for Purple. This is why *Crown Royal Whisky* has successfully used these colors since 1939. The color Blue suggests intelligence, power, respect and authority. Studies have shown that this color is equally respected by men and women. White denotes sophistication, luxury and even mystery. Black is suggestive of calm, and peace. Black is also a safe neutral color to use. The graphic designer you work with for label design should be well versed on the psychology of color.

REFERENCES

www.morebeer.com
www.OntarioBeerKegs.com
www.stpats.com
www.letina.com
www.ripleystainless.com
www.cellartek.com
www.shanleypump.com
www.brennereianlagen.de
www.verder.co.uk
www.alliedhose.ca
www.certuss.com
www.weil-mclain.com
www.prochiller.com
www.lusiancoppers.com
www.copper-alembic.com
www.Hillbillystills.com
www.stilldragon.com
www.coppermoonshinestills.com
www.rockypointcopperstills.com
www.Corsondistilling.com
www.hbscopper.com
www.prosperoequipment.com
www.confederatestills.com
www.artisanstilldesign.com
www.bruniglass.com
www.saverglass.com
www.thinkuniversal.com

9

CLEANING

Bacterial contamination can pose problems for both the home distiller and the craft distiller. Bacteria – like their close relatives of the yeast family – like to consume sugars. Bacteria, however, don't generate alcohols. They can generate unwanted substances such as acetic acid (vinegar).

BACTERIA TYPES

Acetobacter: these bacteria have the ability to convert ethanol into acetic acid in the presence of oxygen. This bacteria was first recognized by Louis Pasteur in 1864. The problem with *Acetobacter* is that it is everywhere. It especially will thrive anywhere that natural sugars are present – like a distillery.

Gluconobacter: take an apple or a pear and leave it sitting on your kitchen countertop. Over time, the fruit will spoil. This is an example of *Gluconobacter* at work. This bacteria is a member of the acetic acid bacteria family and therefore closely related to Acetobacter. There are many strains of Gluconobacter that have been identified and some in fact are beneficial. For example, a species called Gluconobacter Cerevisiae is what gives a glass of Belgian lambic beer some of its characteristic sourness. But for a craft distiller, there is nothing beneficial about a bacteria that can interfere with the fermentation process and impair the alcoholic yields in a distillery.

Lactobacillus: this bacteria has a long list of different strains. Many of these strains live in our digestive tracts which assist our bodies in digesting food. Strains of *Lactobacillus* are used in the products of some yogurts, cheeses, sauerkrauts, kimchis and even sourdough breads. But, distillers are not breadmakers. Lactobacillus can consume sugars and convert them into lactic acids. The net result will be a decreased alcoholic yield for the distiller. Lactobacillus is naturally present in the husks of grain kernels. Be careful when grinding grain that dust does not end up gravitating onto your fermenter tank.

Leuconostoc Meserenteriodes: this bacteria also produces lactic acid, but it is unique in that it can tolerate environments where the sugar content is up to 50 %. One raw material that can easily host this bacteria is molasses.

Zymomonas Mobilis: this is a waterborne bacteria that will consume sugars to produce alcohol. However, it can also produce funky aromas like rotting apples. Definitely not something a craft distiller wants anything to do with.

These various bacteria will survive at pH 3.8 and higher and temperatures of 18 to 30C. This pretty much means that if you are not careful, these bacteria will make an unwanted appearance at your craft distillery.

CLEANING AGENTS

There are several available methods for keeping these creatures at bay.

Caustic Soda (sodium hydroxide): is a particularly good cleaning solution. It has an excellent ability to dissolve caked-on material from tank surfaces, pumps and hoses. It has good rinsability which means a flush with clean water will be sufficient in removing it from tanks, pumps and hoses. Safety is critical when using caustic soda. Be sure to wear a safety visor and also rubber gloves when measuring out caustic for use in a cleaning cycle. A splash of caustic in the face or on the hands can have nasty consequences. There will be vendors in your community that sell industrial cleaning supplies. Speak to them about sourcing a pail of caustic soda. Home distillers interested in using caustic should visit their local hardware store and purchase a box of lye. A water solution containing 4 % lye will prove effective in cleaning. Just remember - safety first.

Javex (sodium hypochlorite): is very effective at killing bacteria. When mixed with water, Javex forms hypochlorous acid. The problem with Javex is that it can lead to pitting on stainless steel surfaces. Craft distillers should avoid using the stuff altogether. Home distillers using plastic fermentation pails can use Javex as a cleaner. Javex is not quite as rinsable as caustic soda. So be sure to give your equipment a few extra water flushes when using this product.

Iodofor (Iodine solution): is effective at killing bacteria. We are all familiar with Iodine and how it can stain. Iodofor is Iodine that has been blended with a high molecular weight substance to help avoid the staining aspect. The concentration of Iodine in an iodofor is 12.5 ppm.

Detergents: are good at cleaning equipment. One detergent cleaner that I have used for many years now is tri-sodium-phosphate which sells under the brand name TSP. You will find TSP in your hardware store in the paint section. It has good rinsability and is good at dissolving caked-on material from surfaces.

Citric Acid: is a distillers best friend for removing sulfide scale buildup inside a still. Citric acid can be purchased in bulk, crystalline form. A solution of 450 grams to 1 liter of water should be adequate.

C.I.P.

Craft distillers when sourcing equipment should budget to have a cleaning-in-place (CIP) system installed on tanks and on still pots and columns. A CIP system essentially consists of a multi-nozzle spray ball positioned inside a tank or a still. Cleaning solution is supplied at high pressure at the spray ball using the mash pump. The cleaning solution sprays from the spray ball at high pressure and impacts all internal surfaces. Once the cleaning solution has been sprayed, the process is repeated using water to rinse.

REFERENCES

How to Brew, John Palmer, 2001, Defenstrative Publishing, USA

10

INSTRUMENTS & PROOFING

Home distillers and craft distillers alike will need the following four instruments – a thermometer, an alcoholmeter, a refractometer and a pH meter.

Thermometer: the thermometer can trace its rudimentary beginnings back to 1593 and the time of Galileo. In the early 1600s, Italian inventor Santorio took Galileo's basic design and added a numerical scale. In 1645, Italian nobleman Ferdinand II developed the first ever liquid-in-glass thermometer. In 1714, German scientist Daniel Fahrenheit improved this design further by using Mercury as the liquid inside the glass. Home distillers can take the easy route and purchase a digital thermometer from their local home brewing store.

Craft distillers in America, however, will have to purchase the standard mercury-in-glass thermometer. The use of thermometers for proofing alcohol in America is governed by 27 CFR part 30, section 22. Depending on the style of thermometer, and there are only four allowed styles, the accuracy will have to be at between 1 degree Fahrenheit and ¼ of a degree Fahrenheit. From time to time appropriate TTB officers shall verify the accuracy of thermometers used by proprietors.

In Canada, craft distillers can use either a mercury-in-glass thermometer or a digital model. Digital models can be prohibitively expensive. A suitable digital unit must be capable of reading temperatures between -25C and +45C with incremental steps of not more than 0.1C. Digital thermometers will have to be examined annually for accuracy. In Canada, The Science and Engineering Directorate (SED) of the Canada Border Services Agency has authority over all instruments used in alcohol proofing. This agency will be the one who does your annual calibrations. Glass thermometers must read between -25C and 45C with 0.5C increments. Glass thermometers, once approved, must be re-examined every five years.

Alcoholmeter (Hydrometer): the hydrometer can trace its origins back to scientists Nicholson an Baume in the mid-1800s. Home distillers can simply purchase a cheap hydrometer from an on-line vendor. I have had good success with Nova-Tech USA based in Texas and routinely use their alcoholmeters in Workshops. I simply place my order on-line and within days my parcel arrives via UPS.

Craft distillers, however, are more tightly regulated. In America, hydrometers are divided into 11 classes, with each class representing a different alcohol proof range. For example, a class L hydrometer shall read between 90 and 110 proof with an accuracy of 0.2 proof. The use of hydrometers in proofing alcohol is governed by 27 CFR part 30, section 22. In America, alcohol strength is expressed in units called *proof*. Hydrometers are calibrated for accuracy at 60 F. Proofing tables must be used if the temperature of the alcohol being proofed differs from 60F. From time to time appropriate TTB officers shall verify the accuracy of hydrometers used by proprietors.

In Canada, alcohol proofing is based on density units of kg/m3. Hydrometers in Canada must have a range of no more than 20 units, so craft distillers will have to purchase a series of hydrometers to cover the range of alcoholic strengths they are dealing with in their distillery. Each hydrometer will cost at least $250. The accuracy of a hydrometer must be +/- 0.2 kg/m^3. Once approved, hydrometers must be re-examined every five years.

Digital units are allowed in Canada, but the accuracy of these units is extremely tight and there is a rigorous procedure for getting a digital unit approved.

Closely related to spirits proofing in Canada is the issue of a weigh scale. In Canada, craft distillers will be required to purchase a digital scale suitable for weighing larger totes of bulk alcohol. Knowing the mass of alcoholic liquid in a bulk tote will then allow the distiller to quickly calculate the volume of absolute alcohol contained in the tote. This data will be required for monthly government reporting purposes. Weigh scales, once approved, will have to be re-certified every two years.

Refractometer: in the early 1800s, scientists Karl Balling, Adolf Brix and Fritz Plato all were developing measuring scales to record the sugar concentration of solutions. Today, the most commonly referred to scale is the Brix scale where 1 degree Brix is the equivalent of 1 gram sucrose in 100 grams of solution.

The optical refractometer comprises a lens and an eyepiece. The user will place several drops of liquid to be tested on the lens and then look through the eyepiece. The scale in calibrated so that with pure water on the lens a reading of 0 will result. Scales on refractometers usually go from 0 to 35 Brix. Drops of sugary solution on the lens will cause light to refract (bend) as it passes the lens. This will cause a shaded line to appear on the scale which the viewer can then read. For both home distillers and craft distillers, refractometers are easy to find. I purchased one for about $120 from an on-line store that retailed scientific instruments.

pH Meter: the first rudimentary pH meter was developed in 1906 by Fritz Haber. In 1936, American scientist Arnold Beckman refined the device. pH is a mathematical construct based on the negative base 10 logarithm of hydrogen ion concentration. The pH scale goes from 1 to 14 with pH 1 being a strong acid and pH 14 being a strong base. Water is around pH 7. pH meters are especially useful for dealing with un-malted grains and artificial enzymes where the pH of your mash should be at the enzyme manufacturers recommended level. pH meters are easily obtainable from on-line retailers of scientific instruments.

American Proofing Tables: In America, 27 CFR part 30 section 62 provides the TTB Gauging Manual. Figure 20 illustrates a portion of this Table.

Consider this short example: If the hydrometer reads 54 proof and the temperature of the solution being proofed is 64F, the true proof strength of the solution being proofed would be 52.3 proof. To convert proof to %age alcohol, simply divide by 2.

46

TABLE No. 1

TRUE PERCENT PROOF

Hydrometer reading	Temperature °F.									
	61°	62°	63°	64°	65°	66°	67°	68°	69°	70°
51	50. 6	50. 2	49. 8	49. 4	49. 0	48. 6	48. 2	47. 8	47. 4	47. 0
52	51. 6	51. 2	50. 8	50. 4	50. 0	49. 6	49. 2	48. 8	48. 4	48. 0
53	52. 6	52. 2	51. 8	51. 4	51. 0	50. 5	50. 1	49. 7	49. 3	48. 9
54	53. 6	53. 2	52. 8	52. 3	51. 9	51. 5	51. 1	50. 7	50. 3	49. 8
55	54. 6	54. 2	53. 7	53. 3	52. 9	52. 5	52. 0	51. 6	51. 2	50. 8

Figure 20 a portion of the TTB Gauging Tables

Canadian Proofing Tables: In Canada, the Canadian Alcoholometric Tables provide the data necessary to proof alcoholic spirits. Figure 21 illustrates a portion of the table.

ALC_TAB - Notepad

File Edit Format View Help

22.5	934.0	1.0698	47.1	0.9980
22.5	934.2	1.0696	46.9	0.9980
22.5	934.4	1.0694	46.8	0.9980
22.5	934.6	1.0692	46.7	0.9980
22.5	934.8	1.0689	46.6	0.9980
22.5	935.0	1.0687	46.5	0.9980
22.5	935.2	1.0685	46.4	0.9980
22.5	935.4	1.0682	46.3	0.9980
22.5	935.6	1.0680	46.2	0.9980
22.5	935.8	1.0678	46.1	0.9980
22.5	936.0	1.0676	46.0	0.9981
22.5	936.2	1.0673	45.9	0.9981
22.5	936.4	1.0671	45.8	0.9981
22.5	936.6	1.0669	45.7	0.9981
22.5	936.8	1.0667	45.5	0.9981
22.5	937.0	1.0664	45.4	0.9981
22.5	937.2	1.0662	45.3	0.9981
22.5	937.4	1.0660	45.2	0.9981
22.5	937.6	1.0658	45.1	0.9981
22.5	937.8	1.0655	45.0	0.9981
22.5	938.0	1.0653	44.9	0.9981
22.5	938.2	1.0651	44.8	0.9981
22.5	938.4	1.0649	44.7	0.9981
22.5	938.6	1.0647	44.6	0.9981

Figure 21 Canadian Excise Tables

Consider the following two examples each using the portion of the Canadian Excise Tables shown in Figure 20.

First, suppose the temperature of the solution being proofed was 22.5C and the hydrometer was reading a density of 936 (which is 0.936 kg/m3). Locate 22.5C in the left hand column and scroll down until you find the density reading of 936.0 in the second column. Move across the table to column 4 and you can see the alcoholic strength of the solution being proofed is 46 % alcohol.

As another example, suppose a craft distiller has a bulk tote containing 200 kgs of alcoholic distillate. The Excise Inspector happens to stop by for an audit and demands to know how much absolute alcohol is contained in the tote. The distiller would measure the temperature of the liquid in the tote and then draw off a sample so as to measure the density. Suppose the temperature was 22.5C and the density was 937.8.

The distiller would multiply the mass (200 kgs) by the figure from column 3 (1.0655) to determine volume in the bulk tote.

200 x 1.0655 = 213.10 liters.

Next, multiply 213.10 by the figure in column 4 which is 45.0 to determine the amount of absolute alcohol in the bulk tote:

213.10 x 045 = 95.895.

The amount of absolute alcohol in the bulk tote is therefore 95.895 liters of absolute alcohol calibrated to 20C.

While these instruments and tables may at first glance appear daunting, they are actually quite easy to use. With a little practice, you will soon become very competent.

U.K. Proofing: The U.K. uses the % alcohol by volume methodology. The Tables used will be similar to the Canadian methodology.

REFERENCES

http://www.cra-arc.gc.ca/E/pub/em/edm1-1-5/edm1-1-5-e.html#_Toc347404444 (or search online for "Excise Canada Alcohol Proofing")

search online for "27 CFR section 30" and you will easily find the relevant legislation

search online for "Canadian Alcoholometric Tables" and you will find the ZIP file containing the table data.

www.novatech-usa.com

11

OAK AGING OF SPIRITS

Wood – what is it? in the chapter called Raw Materials it was pointed out that a molecular chain of glucose molecules was a starch. What then would an extremely long molecular chain of glucose molecules be? The answer is a *cellulose.* Modify a glucose molecule by removing one of the Carbon atoms. Make an extremely long chain of these modified molecules and you would have a *hemi-cellulose.* Bind the cellulose and hemi-cellulose chains together with lignins (organic polymers) , tannins (ellagic acid, gallic acid) and various other organic acids and you have wood.

Whether it is the wood in your oak dining room table or the wood in a baseball bat, the basic molecular structure will involve cellulose, hemicellulose and organic acids all tightly bound together. What differentiates one species of wood from another are the types and amounts of organic acids present and also the size of the *medullary rays* present. Medullary rays run lengthwise along the long axis of a tree. In softwoods such as pine and spruce, these rays are narrow. In hardwoods such as oak, maple, cherry, elm these rays are wide and impart considerable strength to these woods. A long time ago mankind figured out that hardwoods in addition to being strong, had the innate ability to contain liquids. This is why oak wood is such a popular wood for barrel making.

Oak Trees: oak trees grow in two primary regions of the world – North America and Europe. In North America, the most predominant species of oak tree is *Quercus Alba,* otherwise called North American oak. Other species that occur in North America include *Quercus Prinus, Quercus Stellata and Quercus Durandii.* In Europe, the two predominant species of oak are *Quecus Robur* and *Quercus Sessillis.* The main difference between North American oak and

European oak is the organic acids contained in the wood. European oak has a more complex array of acids and will impart a more complex flavor to an alcoholic liquid aged in it.

Barrel Making: oak logs about 30 centimeters in diameter are harvested and taken to a processing mill. The oak logs are cut into quarters and each quarter is then sawn into boards called *staves*. The staves are then dried. It is interesting to note that staves destined for use in barrels that will hold wine are aged outdoors, exposed to the elements for up to two years. Staves destined for barrels that will hold alcoholic spirits are dried in a kiln oven for a short period of time.

The dried staves are then shaped and their edges beveled. The staves are assembled into a cylindrical format and held in place with metal rings, called hoops.

The semi-completed barrel is then exposed to either radiant heat or steam heat. Recall from the chapter on Raw Materials that when a long molecular starch molecule is heated, it starts to break down into smaller units of glucose (sugars). In barrel making, the radiant or steam heat breaks the celluloses and hemicelluloses into smaller sugar units. The more heat applied, the more sugar units that are created. This process is called *toasting*.

Think about your experiences in your kitchen. If you take some sugar in a saucepan and heat it, it turns to caramelized sugar which is dark in color. Barrel makers do something similar. The toasted wood barrels are next lit on fire for a matter of seconds to burn the wood sugars. This process is called *charring*. Charring also causes the lignins, tannins and other organic acids in the wood to change molecular structure. Lignins are altered into phenolic aldehydes, eugenols and guaicols which collectively impart a combination of vanillin, spicy and smoky flavors to any alcoholic liquid that eventually gets aged inside the barrel. The toasting and charring also create esters of carboxylic acid called lactones. Lactones can impart a slight woodiness and fruitiness to the alcoholic spirit that will be aged in the oak barrel. American oak will generate a greater number of lactones upon toasting and charring. The science of the molecules that develop upon toasting and charring is a complex one indeed and scientists continue to investigate the chemistry at work.

Following charring, the barrel hoops are further pressed into place. The barrels are then fitted with tops and bottoms, leak tested and shipped to the waiting distillery. There are a number of excellent YouTube videos that will provide you with the full visual experience of barrel making. These are listed in the Reference section of this chapter.

Reactions: in addition to the distillate placed in an oak barrel absorbing the various organic molecules created during toasting and charring of the barrel, there are a series of chemical reactions that occur once distillate is placed in an oak barrel. These reactions include oxidations, esterifications, Maillard reactions, polymerizations and condensation reactions. As an example of one such reaction, ethanol gradually oxidizes into acetaldehyde and acetic acid and then into ethyl acetate which can reduce the pungency of the spirit and contribute to smoothness. There are in turn, a number of variables that influence these various reactions. The science of oak aging is a complex one indeed.

Storage Conditions: there is an ongoing debate over humidity and temperature storage conditions for oak-barreled alcoholic spirits. If oak barrels containing alcoholic distillate are left in an area of high humidity, water will be impeded from evaporating from the barrel. Alcohol will, however, evaporate and there will be a reduction in alcoholic strength. On the other hand, if oak barrels are left in an area of low humidity, more water than alcohol will evaporate from the barrels.

If the temperature of the storage area is too hot, the delicate flavors of the alcoholic distillate could be impaired resulting in a poorer quality spirit for the craft distiller to sell to his customer. The academic papers I have read suggest that a humidity of about 65 % and a temperature of 20-23C (room temperature) is best. Jeff Arnett, Master Distiller at Jack Daniels in Lynchburg, Tennessee, has a different opinion on temperature. He maintains one of the secrets to *Jack Daniels Tennessee Whisky* is the variation in seasonal temperature which causes the distillate in the oak barrels to expand into and out of the wood staves.

As far as alcoholic strength of the distillate in the oak barrels is concerned, there too opinion differs. Some argue that 55 % alcoholic strength in the barrel is best while others argue that 65 % is best. The American legal definitions for spirits have gone a long way to resolving some of this opinion difference. (recall from the section on Spirit Definitions that Bourbon must be aged in oak at not more than 62.5 % alcohol). Some of the big commercial Whisky makers in Canada load distillate into oak barrels at 75 % strength. I suspect this is in an effort to optimize the number of barrels need for aging. In my travels to craft distilleries, I have found that something around the 63 to 65 % level is common.

Surface to Volume Ratio: the size of the oak barrel is a significant factor in aging. When approximating surface to volume ratio, measure the widest diameter of the barrel and also the height of the barrel. Ignore the fact that the barrel staves have some curvature to them. Use the formula *pi x diameter x height* to calculate the surface area of the barrel. To this figure add *pi x radius squared* to determine the surface area of each of the top and bottom of the barrel. Knowing the volumetric size of the barrel allows you to arrive at the square centimeters per liter surface to volume figure.

Play around with some hypothetical figures and mathematically you will soon see that surface to volume ratio will decline as the volume of the barrel increases. A small barrel of size 20 liters will have a surface to volume ratio of near 195 square centimeters per liter. A barrel of size 200 liters will have a ratio of 90 which is just about half that of the small barrel. This means that a smaller 20 liter barrel, in theory at least, will age an alcoholic spirit in half the time of a 200 liter barrel. This notion is important for home distillers who will be sourcing small barrels of size 10 liters to 20 liters. Do not place alcoholic distillate in small barrels and forget about them for three years. You will be disappointed. Small barrels age spirits faster. Be sure to frequently check the spirit in your small barrel to ensure it is not taking on a woody taste.

Vendors: there are several avenues of approach for home distillers and craft distillers to obtain barrels. I have talked to home distillers who are pleased with the company 1000 Oak Barrels from Manassas, Virginia who make good quality small barrels. A Canadian vendor to consider is Canadian Oak Barrels in Ontario, Canada. Another I have recently heard of is Gibbs Brothers Cooperage in Arkansas.

Another approach is to talk to American small batch craft distillers who are making Bourbon which by law must be aged in charred new oak barrels. Once these barrels have been used once, they usually get sold. One source for barrels is the Woodinville Whisky Company in Washington State, USA. Visit their website to place an order for their used 15 gallon oak barrels.

Full sized 200 liter used barrels will come from the big distillers. Jack Daniels in particular makes its barrels available to craft distillers in limited quantities. However, bear in mind that these barrels may have already been used for up to five years. Jack Daniels makes its own barrels and as such knows how long to toast them and char them for their aging period. As a craft distiller, you run the risk that the organic acids in these barrels may be partly diminished by the time you receive the barrel. You will hear the argument that many Jack Daniels barrels will find their way to the Scotch Whisky makers in Scotland. This argument is true, but bear in mind that Scotch Whisky is a unique product. Place a wonderful smoky, peaty Scotch is a brand new toasted, charred oak barrel and you run the risk of the sugars and organic acids interfering with the taste profile. In this regard, a used oak barrel with diminished character is exactly what the Scotch maker wants. Some Scottish distillers have their own coopers who will tear the barrels apart, apply new ends, then re-toast and re-char the barrels in a process called *rejuvenation.* As a craft distiller, weigh your options carefully. You likely are not about to start rejuvenating used barrels. But, you do want to impart some excellent flavors into your aged spirit. The cost of barrels, both new and used, is rising. But, you may find the price differential between new and used is narrowing significantly. Do your research. Sample different spirits that have been exposed to American oak barrels and European oak barrels, both new and used. You may find that it is more beneficial to purchase new, charred oak barrels.

Another source of barrels is the wine industry. Many winemakers import French oak barrels. After a few uses, these barrels may be discarded. Do your homework. How long has the barrel been used? Is it in need of dis-assembly for re-toasting and re-charring?

If a new barrel is your aim, talk to a manufacturer like The Barrel Mill in Minnesota, USA who will toast and char full sized barrels to various specifications depending on what you the end user wants. Consider also Canadian Oak Barrels, located in St. George, Ontario.

One other avenue to consider is the use of oak chips and small oak sticks in bottles. Exposing toasted oak chips to a newly-made Whisky distillate will impart oak flavor to the distillate. With some experimentation, a craft distiller may discover that it is possible to craft a very nice Whisky that the consumer will enjoy sipping. The notion of small oak sticks placed inside bottles has evolved into a pseudo-science. Black Swan Barrels in Minnesota has developed a honeycomb wood stave (patent pending) that, thanks to its surface area, will quickly impart oak flavors into a distillate. According to their website, exposing three inches of wood stave to one gallon of distillate for six weeks will impart suitable flavor to the spirit. These staves are available in nine different type of wood.

However, in my opinion, one cannot cheat time and chemistry. Yes, a stick in a bottle will impart some flavor to a spirit because alcohol is a solvent and it will extract the organic acids from the stick. But, distillate in an oak barrel will breathe. The reactions inside a barrel are complex and take time to complete. Time is what will produce an exceptional spirit. A stick in a bottle will give you flavor. Oak barreling will give you layers upon layers of flavor. Think about the customer you are trying to win over. Think about the big corporate competitors and some of the excellent Scotches, Bourbons and Canadian Whiskies they offer. Can a stick in a bottle compete? I say not.

REFERENCES

The Role of Organic Acids in Maturation of Distilled Spirits in Oak Casks, John Conner, Journal of the Institute of Brewing, Volume 105, Issue 5, pages 287–291, 1999.

When Will the Wood Run Out?, Dominic Roskrow, Whisky Magazine, Issue 122, September 2014, Paragraph Publishing, UK.

Maturation of Wines and Spirits: Comparisons, Facts and Hypotheses, V. Singleton, American Journal of Enology and Viticulture, vol. 46, no 1, 1995.

Wood Maturation of Distilled Beverages, J. Mosedale, J-L Puech, Trends in Food Science and Technology, vol 9, 1995.
www.woodinvillewhiskeyco.com

www.1000oaksbarrel.com

www.canadianoak.com

www.thebarrelmill.com

www.blackswanbarrels.com

http://youtu.be/r-melNZAthg is an interesting YouTube video showing how the Robinson Stave Company from Kentucky makes oak barrels.

https://youtu.be/PEHsv2LsW5U is an interesting YouTube video showing how the McGinnis Wood Products Company from Missouri makes oak barrels.

http://youtu.be/MvKuaS5H8uQ is an interesting YouTube video of Jeff Arnett (Jack Daniels) speaking about oak aging.

12

MARKETING AND BRANDING

If you are a home distiller, you are your own customer – so no need to worry about marketing. But, if you are intent on becoming a craft distiller, marketing and branding are critical to your success. As I like to remind people in my usual blunt fashion – anyone can make the stuff. But, if you cannot sell it, then you won't have a business.

The science of marketing is focused on the 'wants' of a consumer. Think about some of your recent consumer purchases. Think about your latest purchase of alcoholic spirits. Now think about the decision process that an average consumer goes through when wanting a bottle of alcoholic spirits.

A consumer might want a bottle of alcohol because they are out of stock, they are unhappy with the current brand being used, their lifestyle has changed, an advertisement has convinced them to try a new product or because they have heard about a new craft distillery that has opened up in their town.

There are many reasons why a consumer might want to purchase a bottle of alcoholic spirit. In the quest to satisfy that want of a bottle of spirit, the typical consumer will go through a complex mental evaluation process. As a craft distiller, you want to insert your product into this complex mental evaluation process. The following are critical aspects of your marketing program that relate directly to this process.

The Brand: branding is the art – and it *is* an art – of conveying a unique and compelling message to the consumer. Everything about your product must be unique and compelling. As a craft distiller competing against the big commercial distillers, you have two powerful cards in your poker hand. You are different and you are local. Play these cards strategically and your odds of winning the customer over to your product improve markedly.

What Problem? there are several components that all work together to define your brand. Chief among these is the question of what problem does your product solve. If you can demonstrate to the consumer that your spirit beverage solves a problem, the consumer will seriously consider your product as part of their complex mental evaluation process. I see very few craft distillers who have actually been able to clearly convey a problem solving message. One notable exception is that of Corsair Distilling in Kentucky. Stuck in the middle of a state that produces most of the Bourbon in the world, one would think it would be hard for this craft distiller to stand out. Bourbon has become a much celebrated product and appreciating Bourbon has evolved into something of an art form. So what about the person who is not interested in consulting the latest Bourbon tasting notes in *Whisky Advocate* magazine? What about the average ordinary person? Corsair has reached out to that consumer with a problem solving solution. Corsair uses a very straightforward marketing message to clearly convey its brand. That message is – *Small Batch, Handcrafted Booze for Bad Asses.* This message is catching on in a big way and Corsair is enjoying some very good success.

As you contemplate your craft distillery startup, think about the problems in the world of commercially-made spirits. The big commercial distillers have failed to display much innovation over the past several decades. The big distillers do not focus on individual cities, towns or agricultural areas. The big distillers are often using chemical coloring and flavoring in their products. These are but some of the problems that you could focus on to deftly insert your brand into the mind of the consumer.

Mission and Vision: we all like to follow people who are on a journey. We like to be part of that journey. What mission will you be on as a craft distiller? What is your vision for the future?

Some years ago Jet Blue Airways unveiled its vison and mission to the air travelling consumer when it said Jet Blue was dedicated to bringing humanity back to air travel. To any consumer wanting to book an airline ticket, this is a powerful statement especially if that consumer has had a bad travel experience lately.

I have seen very few craft distillers clearly convey a mission and a vision. One example of a compelling mission statement is the Toronto Distilling Company in Toronto, Canada. They clearly state they are intent on distilling the agricultural bounty of Ontario, a diverse agricultural area with many different crops being grown. When someone claims they are intent on distilling the agricultural bounty of Ontario, this implies they are on a journey that will take some time and quite likely provide many exciting opportunities. As a curious consumer, I know I would be interested in following the Toronto Distilling Company on its mission. I would be tempted to visit their distillery quite often to see what new products they have created.

Another example of a good mission and vision statement comes from the Santa Fe Distilling Company in Santa Fe, New Mexico. This craft distillery has stated it is intent on creating the most intriguing and delicious expressions of premium desert spirits the world has ever known. That's quite a vision, quite a mission. As a consumer who enjoys unique alcoholic spirits, this is a craft distillery I would certainly follow.

Your USP: as a consumer's mind computes data to determine which spirit drink will satisfy the want that is to be satisfied, it helps if you can present the consumer with a Unique Selling Proposition (USP).

A good example of a USP comes from the world of Tequila. The world is full of Tequila and most of it is made in large institutional, mass-production distilleries. Arrogante Tequila was seeking to break into the American marketplace and it did so with its unique philosophy. Arrogante said that it made its Tequila using only traditional stone ovens and that preserving and honoring traditional craftsmanship was the cornerstone of their business. It worked. Consumers shifted to Arrogante Tequila in large numbers because of this unique perspective.

I have come across many other examples of great USPs in my research. Sacred Spirits in England sets itself apart from other craft Gin makers by promoting its use of vacuum distillation of 12 individual botanicals. The resulting individual distillates are then blended according to a tried and true recipe. Kings County Distillery in New York State makes mention of using traditional Copper stills fabricated in Scotland, wooden fermenter vessels made by local craftsmen and the use of corn and barley grown locally. But, they really hit a home run when they mentioned that they are a model of traditional and sustainable Whisky production.

While I have come across many powerful USPs in my research, many craft distillers have simply failed to convey a USP. Just because you open a craft distillery, does not mean consumers will flock to your front door. Start thinking about what makes your craft distillery unique. This may not be an easy process. It may take time and many iterations.

Emotions: what emotions do you wish to convey to your customer? Think about some mainstream brand names and the emotions they convey. Think Volvo cars and how they convey a message of rugged dependability. Think Disney and its emotions of happiness and excitement. The colors you select on your labels, the weight of your bottles, the shape of your bottles and even the name of your spirit will factor into the emotions you want the customer to feel. One excellent example of emotion comes from a craft distillery in Vancouver, Canada called Odd Society Spirits. The very name implies a welcoming place (a society) for people who do not necessarily fit the norm (odd). In other words, a place for people who like something other than Vodka and orange juice. Combine the name Odd Society with some seriously quirky artwork in the tasting room and on the bottle labels and you have a winning combination.

Another outstanding example comes from The Moonshine Company in Paducah, Kentucky. When you walk in the door you are greeted by the congenial character, Cousin Billy. The tasting area is filled with artwork from the Prohibition era along with many old stills and condensers from decades ago. Wrap all this up in Cousin Billy's stories about making 'shine back home in Tennessee for 56 years and you have the complete emotional experience. I could not help but notice that customers were walking out with multiple bottles of Moonshine under their arms and big grins on their faces. As far as the product itself is concerned – I must admit this was by far and away the best Moonshine I had on my travels through Tennessee and Kentucky.

Start thinking about what kind of emotion you want your craft distillery to convey. It will take you a lot of time to properly define this emotion. Engage family and friends in the process. Visit other craft distilleries in the process. Draw the consumer towards you with emotion.

Personality: this is somewhat related to emotion. Think IBM and what sort of personality comes to mind? Stable, blue chip, establishment-man to name a few. Now take a visit to the website for Hendricks Gin and assess the personality on offer. Quirky, weird, bizarre are a few descriptors that come to mind.

Delivery of Identity: as you make progress on the above items, think about how you will deliver that brand message. Energizer batteries for decades has been using the iconic pink bunny rabbit. Frosted Flakes breakfast cereal has been using Tony the Tiger ever since I can remember (and I have been around for a handful of decades). Nike uses the iconic swoosh with the three words *Just Do It.* Very powerful. All you have to see is the swoosh symbol to know the product has been made by Nike.

In the world of spirits, Maker's Mark Bourbon is noted for its iconic red wax seal. In Canada, one good example can be found at Urban Distilleries in Kelowna, British Columbia. This craft distillery is renowned across Canada for its Spirit Bear Gin and Spirit Bear Vodka. The brand identity is conveyed with the image of a bear's head on every bottle. Very powerful indeed.

Figure 22 - Conveying the brand image for Urban Distilleries

What's In a Name? hard to believe, but picking a name for your craft distillery will be more challenging than you think.

You can settle on a geographical name such as Yaletown Distilling which suggests it is located in the Yaletown area of Vancouver, Canada. All fine and good if you are from Vancouver. But what if you are from a different city or different country? Will this name resonate with you?

You can pick a theme-based name. For example, Big Rig Distilling in Edmonton, Canada has picked a name that aligns with the product that provides much of the economic activity for the area – oil. Legend Distilling in Naramata, British Columbia picks a different local legend or phenomenon for each of its spirits. Its Doctor's Orders Gin hearkens back to the Prohibition era when you needed a doctor's note to acquire a bottle of alcoholic beverage. Its Shadow in the Lake Vodka refers to the mystical creature *Ogopogo* that many say lives in the nearby lake.

You can pick an individual name for each of your spirits where each name has a story that celebrates something. The various names for your products need not all be alignment with each other. For example, Odd Society Spirits in Vancouver, Canada has its Wallflower Gin which is described as being a shy, introverted product. Its East Van Vodka is a celebration of the East Vancouver community. Yukon Shine Distilling in Whitehorse, Canada has two products – its Yukon Winter Vodka is a reference to Yukon winters which can be quite crisp and bracing. Its Aura Gin is a celebration of the spectacular Northern Lights, *Aurora Borealis,* which are a marvel to behold. As you start developing a naming strategy for your craft distillery and your products, don't be discouraged if it takes you considerable time to complete the task.

Juggling the Balls: One book that may assist you in your efforts with all of the above items is *Fired Up – From Corporate Kiss-Off to Entrepreneurial Kick-Off* by Michael Gill and Sheila Paterson. If you are starting to think that marketing might be more work than you had bargained for – you may be right. Running a small business is like juggling several balls in the air and marketing is a very heavy ball to juggle. Give thought to going into the craft distilling business with a partner who can help you juggle the balls. The book *The E-Myth* by Michael Gerber gives good advice and examples of small businesses that failed because the entrepreneurs starting them tried to juggle all the balls alone.

Information Overload: Think about your day to day experiences as a customer. How many TV stations do you get at your house? How many radio stations can you list off that are broadcasting in your community? How many magazines do you see on a daily basis either at your home or at your office? How many signs and billboards do you see as you drive down the streets of your community? How many flyers are stuffed into your morning paper? The sad reality is, the consumer is utterly overloaded with information.

Studies have suggested that consumers are exposed to some 1500 bits of advertising information each day. We are only able to retain knowledge of about 75 of these bits of data at the end of the day. This chilling statistic serves to underscore the importance of this chapter. As the consumer progresses through the mental evaluations towards making a decision that will satisfy his or her product wants, it is vitally important that your information be among those 75 bits of data that the customer's brain retains each day.

PSYCHOLOGICAL MODELS

Getting your data to stick with the consumer is not a random chance event. There is considerable science behind it. Read books on retail marketing and you will soon see that there are several psychological models being used by big brand name players, including large commercial distilling companies like Jim Beam Global, Diageo and Pernod Ricard. The good news is – you too can use a model to assist you with getting your message to stick with the consumer.

The model that I rely on when assisting entrepreneurs with craft distilling start-ups is called *Neuro Linguistic Programming*, or NLP for short. This model was developed in the early 1970s in California by John Grinder and Richard Bandler.

Proactive and Reactive: the NLP Model says there are Proactive People and Reactive People. Approximately 60 % of us can be either reactive or proactive, depending on the situation, depending on the type of day we are having and depending on our psychological makeup. The remainder of us are equally split between being reactive all of the time and being proactive all of the time. A proactive person likes to jump in and get the task underway. A reactive person will tend to look around and see what others are doing before making a decision.

By incorporating both proactive and reactive words into marketing slogans and image taglines, a craft distiller can reach out and touch both of these psychological groups. Proactive words include: go for it, just do it, jump in, why wait?, get it done, take charge, it's time. Reactive words include: think about it, now that you have tasted it, you might wish to, what would happen if, consider this. I recently had a discussion with a friend of my wife's whom I know is a reactive person. When the topic of discussion turned to Vodka, she informed me that for two decades now she has only ever drank Stolichnaya Vodka. Pulling an NLP phrase from my arsenal, I remarked ' so what would happen if you tasted a craft distilled Vodka that was as good as Stolichnaya?' She agreed to sample some *Triticale Vodka* from Park Distilling in Banff, Alberta that I have in my collection. She was impressed (and so was I – this NLP stuff really works).

Recently I could not help noticing an advertisement for careers in the Canadian Armed Forces that appeared in a magazine recently. The tag line read – *Think About It.* This ad suggests that the Armed Forces are not looking for the impetuous 18 year old with an itchy trigger finger who wants to shoot bad guys. They want people with a sense of reason who can make proper decisions. In other magazines, I found an ad for Lamb's Rum with the proactive tagline – *Plunder the Night.* An ad I found for Smirnoff Coconut Vodka had the proactive tagline – *Crack it Open.* Clearly these spirit brand names are after proactive people who will make a buying decision based on these action type words.

Internal and External: The NLP Model posits that there are Internal people and External People. About 40 % of people are internal all of the time and 40 % of us are external all of the time. The remainder of us can shift between internal and external depending on the situation at hand and our psychological makeup. Internal people like to gather data and then make a decision. External people will depend on the opinions of others when making a decision. Internal words include: you be the judge, take one for test drive today, try it for yourself and see, see what you think, you might consider. External words include: others will notice, studies show, experts say, approved by.

A recent magazine ad for Jaguar cars pictured a Jaguar car parked beside a Mercedes. The tag line had the word *Rich* positioned atop the Mercedes and the word *Chic* positioned over the Jaguar. The implication is that if you drive a Mercedes others will see you as being rich. If you drive a Jaguar you will be seen as being chic. This ad was aimed square at the external person.

A series of ads I am sure you have seen show actor George Clooney with the Nespresso coffee maker. Attach Clooney's image to this coffee maker and external people will trip over each other to pay $200 in a retail store to get one. Such is the power of psychology in advertising. The ads for Smirnoff Double Black Vodka with their simple, but effective tagline – *Step Up* are another example of external wording. This product is aimed at the external person with the implication that if they buy this product it will help them to step up and be noticed by others.

A recent ad for Jack Daniels Honey Whisky stated – *We've Had This Idea on Ice for a While. See what You Think.* This ad is aimed at the internal person who is perhaps more analytical than an external person. This is a new product for Jack Daniels and arguably a departure from its flagship Old No. 7 product. They want people to carefully analyze it. (There is one more subtle hint embedded too. The word 'ice' is suggesting their Honey Whisky is best served on the rocks).

Differences: The NLP Model says 5 % of people are Sameness people. They are not going to change no matter what. My 82 year old mother-in-law drinks Wiser's Whisky and no other brand. I have tried to entice her to try different Whisky's. No way, no how – she is not changing. She is part of the 5 % of people who are Sameness oriented. As a craft distiller, be aware that this segment exists and no matter how hard you try, they will never make the shift to craft distilled products.

About 20 % of us are Difference people. This segment is always on the lookout for new and innovative products. I recently saw an ad for careers in the Canadian Armed Forces. The tagline read – *Careers With a Difference.* The Armed Forces has no interest in people who want to remain in one location forever. They want people who are willing to be transferred to different military bases. By using psychological language in the ad, they are pre-filtering the applicants without having to read application forms or perform interviews on inappropriate candidates.

I regularly experiment with different infusions in alcohol. I have had good success with tea infused Gin, which was quite popular in England in the early 1900s. Tea infused Gin is without doubt a different type of product. If I were starting a craft distillery, tea infused Gin would be one of my flagship products. A tagline that reads – *Afternoon Tea, Redefined* might draw the attention of that segment who enjoys different products.

About 65 % of us will try a new product as long as we perceive that it is not too far different from what we are drinking at the present time. There have been a few monumental brand name failures where companies failed to recognize this. In the late 1980s, Saturn unveiled a line of cars with the marketing tagline – *A Different Kind of Car.* Consumers ran away screaming. They did not want a different kind of car. They wanted a car with four wheels that could safely and efficiently get them to where they wanted to go. The Saturn brand name is no longer around. Remember when Coke unveiled its New Coke? Devoted Coke drinkers were scared witless with suggestions of a great new taste, better than ever. It took Coke years to claw back lost market share from its rivals.

A classic example of a spirit brand not shocking customers is Crown Royal's Maple Flavored Whisky and Apple Flavored Whisky. The bottle shape is the same as the regular Crown Royal. The iconic gold cap is still there. The crown and purple pillow are still on the label. The box shape is the same and the iconic cloth bag with drawstrings is still present, just in a different color. Diageo fully understands the dangers in shocking the customer out of his or her comfort zone.

I recently saw an ad for Wiser's Whisky with the tagline – *Distilled, Aged and Blended the Same Way Since 1857.* The message here is that there is no need to worry. This Whisky has not changed. In late 2015, Wiser's launched two new products, obviously aimed at that segment who enjoys change. One product is its Hopped Whisky, which takes a page right out of JP Wiser's original recipe book from the mid-1800s. The next is its Double Still Rye Whisky – a blend of Whisky from a pot still and a column still. Wiser's recognizes that the marketplace is psychologically divided. Instead of selling one product across all divisions, Wiser's is crafting products and marketing programs for various psychological segments.

As a craft distiller, be aware that the large commercial distillers are using psychological wording in their ads. Tailor your advertising accordingly.

In 2015, I visited the Moonshine Company in Paducah, Kentucky and one product I really enjoyed was their Loaded Lemon Moonshine. If I were a craft distiller making a lemon flavored spirit, I would aim my marketing at those who enjoy change with a tagline that read *Lemon Moonshine - a New Twist.* In late 2015, I met an entrepreneur who was busy setting up a craft distillery in British Columbia, Canada. He is planning to target that growing segment of the marketplace who are resentful at how large established corporations are getting a chokehold on our economy and our way of life. He was playing around with marketing taglines and imagery that squarely criticized the establishment and the *one percenters* who run the establishment. I look forward to seeing what taglines he eventually settles on.

In early 2015, while visiting Topp's Liquor Store in Tempe, Arizona I spotted a product made by Greenbar Distilling in California called Slow Hand 6 Woods Whisky. This Whisky was aged in wood, as Whisky should be. But, the Whisky had been exposed to six types of wood during the aging process. Different, yes. But it was still wood aged, and not radically different enough to scare people away.

Options and Procedures: The NLP Model says that about 40 % of us are Options based and 40 % of us are Procedures based. The reminder of us can fall into either category. Options words include:

possibilities, sky's the limit, something new, an alternative to. Procedures words include: tried and true, chill and serve, just add ice. One company that squarely focuses on the Options person is the hamburger chain Fuddruckers. This chain is famous for cooking you a burger and then giving you free run of a wide variety of condiments to complete the construction of your burger to your personal liking.

A company that focuses on the Procedures person is Ikea. Buy a box of parts from Ikea and with the help of an instruction manual and a screwdriver you can, step by step, build yourself a new dining room table.

I recently saw an ad for Smirnoff Double Black Vodka with images of various fruits and mixes. The tagline – *A Few More Suggestions on How to Best Bring Out the Taste of Smirnoff Black*. Notice the language - A Few More Suggestions - implies that there are many more options available to the end user of this Vodka beyond those that appear in this ad. Clearly Smirnoff is aimed at the segment that like option when experimenting with their Vodka.

As you create a website for your craft distillery, be sure to include a section containing cocktail and food recipes. Include some cocktail and food pairing suggestions but also some detailed step by step cocktail and food recipes. Target both the Options person and the Procedures person.

Representational Systems: The NLP Model says that people have different ways of processing words and images in advertising. Some 29 % of people use a visual system. That is, when they see an ad, they tend to imagine themselves with the product in that ad. The shape of the bottle, the color of the label and the 'look' of the beverage in the bottle will all be important. This is sometimes called using ones 'mind's eye'.

A similar percentage of us use a kinesthetic process to evaluate data. How a person feels, a change in their body temperature, a warm fuzzy feeling or a tingle up the spine will direct the decision whether or not to buy the bottle of distilled spirit pictured in the ad.

About 11 % of people use an auditory system. When faced with an ad, an auditory person will listen to that little voice in the back of their head that directs them whether or not to purchase. They may even replay the advertising song or jingle in the back of their head as they consume the spirit beverage.

But, nature likes variety and that is why studies have shown that about 37 % of us will use a combination of two of these systems to evaluate and process advertising data.

For example, an ad phrase for your craft distilled Gin that reads – *Take Charge of Your Martini* will be effective when aimed at the Proactive person. Modify this phrase to read *Look How You Can Take Charge of Your Martini.* Now you have something that appeals to Proactive people who use either in part or in whole a visual system to analyze data. As another example, take this same phrase and modify it to read *Take Charge of Your Martini. Experience Some Today.* The word 'experience' will cause the Proactive person using a Kinesthetic system to be drawn to this Gin product. A classic example of kinesthetic words comes from Captain Morgan Rum with its tagline – *Got a Little Captain in You?* We all like to fancy ourselves at some level to be the swashbuckling pirate. It sends shivers up our spines. Get this Rum and be your own pirate.

Towards and Away From: The NLP Model says that about 40 % of us are towards people and 40 % of us are away from people. The remaining 20 % of us can fall into either camp depending on the situation and our individual makeup. Away from words include: won't have to, solve, prevent, block, fix, avoid, eliminate. Towards

words include: attain, obtain, have, get, achieve, enable, accomplish, and advantage.
A powerful example of this language comes from heartburn pill brand Prilosec OTC. Their ads state *Block the Acid. Don't Get Heartburn in the First Place.* If you are a heartburn sufferer, are you going to run towards this product? Indeed you are. Now, wrap this ad with the ever hilarious Larry the Cable Guy and his *Get 'er done, Get 'er accomplished* comedy line and you have a winning ad campaign.

When it comes to craft distilled spirits, think about what problems you can solve. Many brand name Vodka products are not smooth enough to sip straight up. With some clever wording, you can reach out to people and remind them that your craft distilled Vodka will help them avoid the harsh burn.

A powerful example of an ad campaign that draws people towards comes from Bulleit Rye and Bulleit Bourbon. This brand was started by Tom Bulleit who engaged a contract distiller called MGP Products to create a Whisky and a Bourbon for him. He wrapped these products in a story about how he risked everything he had, quit his job and went on a mission to revive the old recipes used by his great-grandfather Augustus Bulleit. At some level, we are attracted to the entrepreneur who risked it all or to the poker player who went all-in and won the tournament. If we cannot be that person, then at least we can buy their product. The Bulleit brand became so successful with this clever marketing that drinks giant Diageo bought the entire brand name.

Alternatively, there is a small craft distiller in Saskatoon, Canada called Lucky Bastard. They have opted to employ images of scantily clad women on their labels. I have talked to many women about this imagery and have yet to find one woman who is thrilled by it. This is a classic example of how images (never mind the words) can send people running away.

While on the topic of image, you may have noticed recently that some craft distillers are using the classic mason jar for their products. This jar transports us back in time to grandma's kitchen when the world was arguably a kinder, gentler place. So, even the type of container you choose for your product can set off psychological reactions in people that can make them move towards your product.

Private Label Products: one way of endearing people to you and your craft distilled spirits is to make them feel special. As you create your craft distillery, look around your community for organizations or events that you can reach out to. Are there annual music or cultural festivals? Are there annual sporting events? Are there service clubs?

One example of this strategy is a distillery in Scotland that decided to target the various Masonic Lodges in its geographic area. They crafted a Whisky called Old Masters Whisky and continue to enjoy success selling it to Masons. I found a unique example at Topp's Liquor Store in Tempe, Arizona. George Dickel Distilling took some of its nine year old Whisky and simply added a small Copper tag and chain around the neck of each bottle. Each Copper tag read *Bottled Exclusively for Topp's Liquor, Tempe, Arizona.* Do you have any private liquor stores in your area? What about corporate events? Without changing your labels, you could make up some of these copper tags that read *Bottled Exclusively for ABC Oil Company Management Golf Tournament 2016.*

The sky is the limit when it comes to private labelling. Think outside the box. Imagine the possibilities. People will notice a private labelled product. Try private labelling and see for yourself.

Refer to the Experts: The NLP Model is a lot deeper than just what I have alluded to in this chapter. For additional reading, I suggest getting a book by international NLP expert, Shelly Rose Charvet. She travels the world consulting to the big brand names and she assists them in using NLP words to drive consumer sales. Her book *Words That Change Minds* is an excellent read. Another author I have discovered is Lou Larsen. His books, *Extreme Language Patterns* and *The World's Most Powerful Written Persuasion Techniques* are both good resources to deepen your NLP understanding.

REFERENCES

Words That Change Minds, Shelley Rose Charvet, Success Strategies, USA,1997. www.successstrategies.com

Extreme Language Patterns, Lou Larsen, 2011, USA.

The World's Most Powerful Written Persuasion Techniques, Lou Larsen, 2013, USA

Fired Up, Michael Gill, Sheila Paterson, Penguin Books, 1998, Australia.

The E-Myth, Michael Gerber, Harper Collins, 2004, USA.

13

REGULATORY REQUIREMENTS

Every country and every jurisdiction within that country will have its own unique requirements for establishing a craft distillery. In this chapter, you will find described to the best of my ability the basic requirements for a wide array of locations. Bear in mind that slowly but surely government regulators are relaxing their stance towards spirit beverages. As you set about planning your craft distillery, it is prudent to first meet face to face with the regulators in your state, province, municipality or council and determine the most recent legislative requirements.

Canada: in Canada, a craft distiller is required to obtain two licenses from the Government of Canada, Excise Department. The first will be a spirits license, which will allow you to produce alcoholic spirits. The second will be a warehouse license which will allow you to possess alcohol that you have not yet paid duties to Excise Canada on. The federal duties in Canada are $11.696 per liter of absolute alcohol. As an example, a 750 ml bottle of 40 % alcoholic strength contains 0.750 x 0.40 = 300 mls of absolute alcohol. The duties owing to the Canadian Government are calculated as:

0.300 x $11.696 = $3.50.

For more details, consult the Excise Canada website at http://www.cra-arc.gc.ca/E/pub/em/edm2-1-1/edm2-1-1-e.html.

Surety Bonds: In Canada, it is required by law that a craft distiller obtain a surety bond to cover unpaid duties on spirits held in bulk. Surety Bonds can be obtained through an insurance company. For example, if a craft distiller had 4000 liters of bulk Whisky aging in oak barrels and if each oak barrel was at a strength of 70 % alcohol, there would be 2800 liters of absolute alcohol contained in the barrels. The duty owing on that alcohol is $11.696 x 2800 = $32,749. Therefore, a surety bond for at least that amount would have to be in place. In the event of theft or other catastrophic loss, Excise Canada would receive the funds from the surety bond to cover the duties owing. Think of a Surety Bond as an insurance policy with Excise Canada as the beneficiary.

United States: in America, a craft distiller is required to obtain a Distilled Spirits Plant license (a DSP license) from the Alcohol and Tobacco tax and Trade Bureau, otherwise called the TTB. The application process is conducted on-line. For more details, consult http://www.ttb.gov/applications/#Manufacturers. The duty owing to the United States Government is $13.50 per proof gallon, where a proof gallon is one gallon of alcohol at a strength of 100 proof (50 %). On a standard 750 ml bottle with 40 % alcohol, the amount owing is $2.14.

United Kingdom: in the UK, a craft distiller is required to obtain a Distillers License from HM Revenue & Customs National Registration Unit located in Glasgow. You will also be required to apply for approval of the plant and processes you intend to use in the manufacturing process. This will include details as to a description of the vessels to be used and a description of the process to be used. For more details, consult https://www.gov.uk/distillers-license-plant-approval. In the UK, the duty owing on a liter of absolute alcohol is a hefty 27.66 Pounds.

The following information relates to the various Canadian Provinces:

Newfoundland: there are at present no craft distilleries in Newfoundland that I am aware of. I have talked to the provincial regulators and they are willing to consider meeting with anyone who wishes to seek application. Prior to meeting with the province, you will be required to obtain approvals from your town or city where you wish to establish your distillery. The province will seek a tax on spirits produced of $17.57 per liter of finished product. On a standard 750 ml bottle, this will be $13.17 owing to the province over and above the $3.50 that would be owing to the Government of Canada.

Nova Scotia: in Nova Scotia, the government website advises that you must make application and it must include items such as: floor plans and site of the proposed distillery, location of your retail store, the legal structure of company and a listing of management and Board of Directors personnel. You must also detail products to be produced, alcoholic strength, method of distribution, size and type of containers, production volumes, quality control (including the type of testing equipment you plan to use, how you plan to test the alcohol strength in your product, what lab you plan to use to test the product for alcohol content and safety, your water source, water test results if using a well, cleaning and sterilization process and cleaning schedule.). Details will be required as to the number of people to be employed, capital costs and written approval from your city/town zoning department. You must also ensure that your jurisdiction is not a dry county – apparently some do exist yet in Nova Scotia. Lastly, you must include a copy of your Excise Canada Licenses. A craft distillery in Nova Scotia is capped at 75,000 liters of finished product per year. If you are planning on having a tasting room at your location, you must also obtain necessary approvals from your Fire Marshall. If there is any good news in this rigorous procedure it is that in 2014 the Nova Scotia Government dropped the provincial markups from 160 % down to between 60 and 80 % for craft distillers Further reductions of 10 % are available if the distiller uses Nova Scotia agricultural products to make the alcohol.

New Brunswick: in New Brunswick it is possible to start a craft distillery with proper approvals from the government. A craft distiller will have to produce less than 75,000 liters of finished product per year. The province apparently applies a flat rate markup on spirits. Beyond this, it is as clear as mud. I find it astounding how some provinces cannot manage to clarify procedures for entrepreneurs seeking to start a business.

Quebec: this is a very difficult jurisdiction to deal with if you are contemplating starting a craft distillery. For starters, you will not be allowed to have a tasting room at your distillery. All your product will be retailed by Societe des Alcools Quebec (SAQ) in their network of retail stores. In order to get your product onto SAQ shelves you will have to submit detailed data on price, quality, brand imagery, sales strategies and more. The price you supply your spirits to SAQ at will be severely marked up so that by the time your product hits store shelves it will be costly for the retail customer. This means that as a distiller, the price you will sell your product to SAQ at will be low. This will have significant adverse impacts on your cash flows.

As an example, consider Montreal-based Cirka Distillers. If you are considering starting a craft distillery in Quebec, I advise taking time to speak with Paul Cirka about his many challenges in dealing with SAQ. One big challenge came after SAQ chemically analyzed Cirka's Vodka and concluded that it exhibited too much flavor and therefore was not in compliance with the Federal definitions for Vodka. It took considerable effort on Mr. Cirka's part to educate SAQ that his product was a true craft made Vodka made from grain and therefore would have some elements of flavor. Apparently SAQ was only accustomed to seeing neutral grain spirits product which is devoid of any subtle flavors.

There is a different angle that some potential craft distillery start-ups in Quebec are investigating. In 2015 I met an entrepreneur from Quebec who is interested in setting up a craft distillery in Quebec City. He plans to sell absolutely zero product to SAQ. He will instead 'export' his products to Alberta, Saskatchewan and other Canadian provinces.

Ontario: like its neighbor, Quebec, Ontario regulations are difficult to deal with. Thanks to some legal wrangling in 2015 by the craft distilling community, a craft distiller can now have a tasting room. But all product sold, whether through a tasting room or not is de facto deemed to be property of the Ontario government who demands a 141 % markup tax in addition to the Excise Canada taxes of $3.50 per bottle. For further clarity, see the website www.doingbusinesswithLCBO.com. LCBO, by the way, stands for Liquor Control Board of Ontario. LCBO will demand extensive data from a craft distiller as to product detail, brand imagery, marketing tactics and sales strategies. Failure to maintain sales levels at the LCBO stores that carry your product will mean almost certain de-listing. I advise Ontario entrepreneurs to first start selling product from their distillery tasting rooms and then move on to seek an LCBO listing once they have a customer following.

Manitoba: Manitoba legislation makes it possible to start a craft distillery with maximum output of 50,000 liters per year. Up until late 2015, there was a provincial markup of 153 % imposed. For craft distillers, this is being slashed to something near 80 % in 2016.

Saskatchewan: Saskatchewan is currently undergoing a serious make-over in its liquor policy. Up until May 2016, policy allowed for craft distilled products to be sold at a markup of 113 % through SLGA retail stores. A craft distiller seeking to sell through his or her tasting room could sidestep this markup and pay only $0.70 per liter plus a 10 % alcohol tax. Of the 75 liquor stores in the Province, up to 40 will soon be privatized. There will be some changes forthcoming on the mark-up of craft spirits sold through these retail stores. Policy currently allows for craft distillers to sell a separate and distinct product to pubs, bars and restaurants at aa lower price point than product sold in retail liquor stores. It is rumored that this will be extended to the big commercial distillers as well. Before launching ahead with a craft distillery project in Saskatchewan, be sure to investigate all the policies carefully.

Alberta: there are only a handful of craft distillers in Alberta at the moment, but the numbers are growing. Alberta requires the usual licenses and applications that other Provinces have and there will be a flat rate markup fee of $13.76 per liter of finished product. On a 750 ml bottle of 40 % strength alcohol, this amounts to $10.32.

British Columbia: this province some time ago took the lead on the craft distilling movement with its BC Craft Distilling Legislation. There will be no provincial markup applied to craft distilled spirits provided that the alcohol is made from 100 % BC grown agricultural product. For many of the craft distillers I have met in BC, this is a welcome bit of legislation.

This also explains why right now there are near 40 craft distillers in BC. This figure represents half the number of craft distillers in all of Canada. But, this legislation is also restrictive. Sugar cane does not grow in BC, so a craft distiller seeking to make Rum is out of luck. There is also only one malting plant in BC – Gambrinus Malting in Armstrong, BC. Source your malted Barley from anywhere else, and you will be in violation of the Craft Distilling Agreement.

The following presents information I have gathered from various US States.

Alabama: There are several craft distillers now operating in Alabama, so getting approvals does not appear to be an issue so long as you are in a 'wet' county. The issue at present seems to be the 56 % state tax levied on product distributed through the State Liquor Board. Lobbying efforts are underway to modify the requirements of

Code of Alabama 28-3-200.

Alaska: In mid-2014, the Alaska legislature passed House Bill 309 which effectively brought craft distilleries on par with craft breweries and wineries in terms of being able to offer tasting to patrons and in terms of being able to conduct some direct sales to bars and restaurants. State taxation rates in Alaska are $2.54 on a standard 750 ml bottle. As of January 2016, there are reportedly five craft distilleries operating in Alaska.

Arizona: the Arizona Department of Liquor Licenses and Control will govern your application for a state craft distilling license allowing you to make up to 20,000 gallons of product per year. The state will allow you to open one remote tasting and retail premise. If your annual output is less than 1,189 gallons you may sell and ship your product directly to Arizona retailers and also residents. Arizona Revised Statutes (ARS) section 4, part 205 is the governing legislation. The state tax on alcohol is a modest $3 per gallon. Craft distillers with output above 1,189 gallons must ship directly to licensed wholesalers in the State.

Arkansas: craft distilling in Arkansas is very much in its infancy yet. The Arkansas Department of Finance and Administration, Title 1, subtitle c(14) allows for a craft distiller to sell to wholesalers, to export out of state and to sell for off-premises consumption. It is probably just a matter of time before small distillers start springing up across the state. State liquor taxes are about $2.50 per gallon.

California: Assembly Bill No. 1295 went into effect January 1, 2016 and with it, craft distilling in the state was given a huge boost. The Alcoholic Beverage Control Act now allows craft distillers to sell up to 2.25 liters per day per person at a tasting room. A person visiting your tasting room can enjoy up to six one-quarter ounce tastings per day. You can also provide mixed cocktails at your tasting room.

Liquor taxes in California are $3.30 per gallon. Craft distillers will be limited to 100,000 gallons per year of output, excluding brandy. At the beginning of 2016 there were just over 50 craft distillers in California.

Colorado: there were about 22 craft distilleries operating in Colorado as of the start of 2016. If you are of good moral character, solid background and have not been funded by unlawful money, you can apply to the Colorado Liquor Authorities for a distilling license under Colorado Revised Statutes, Article 47, Title 12, section 402. You must make separate application to your local municipality for creating a retail tasting room. A wholesalers license will further allow you to sell your products to retailers. Colorado is now examining legislation that would allow for distillery pubs to be created.

Connecticut: in early 2014, House Bill 5429 allowed for the creation of a craft distilling permit process. A craft distiller can make up to 25,000 gallons per year. Samples can be given to the retail public in an amount not exceeding two ounces per person per day. Your place of manufacture must be approved by the Department of Consumer Protection before a distilling permit will be issued. As of January 2016 there were about five craft distillers in the State. State alcohol tax is $5.40 per gallon.

Delaware: Delaware Code Title 4, Chapter 5, sections 512, 546 and 709 govern craft distillers. Craft distillers are exempt from having to shut down on Sundays. Craft distillers can sell up to 12 bottles to a given customer on a given day.

Florida: Florida Statute Title 34, Chapter 565 governs craft distillation. Craft distillers have to make less than 75,000 gallons per year. An annual license fee of $4000 must be paid. State alcohol taxes are $6.50 per gallon. A craft distiller can have a tasting room provided it is located contiguous to the location where the spirits are produced.

A rigorous assessment of the tasting room will be conducted by authorities. A craft distillery may only sell spirits in face-to-face sales transactions with consumers who are making a purchase of no more than:

a. Two individual containers of each branded product; or

b. Three individual containers of a single branded product and up to one individual container of a second branded product; or

c. Four individual containers of a single branded product.

No craft distiller shall ship products to consumers. All sales must be on a face to face basis.

These apparent restrictions probably explain why there are only 14 craft distilleries in such a populous state.

Georgia: in early 2015, Georgia passed State Bill 63. But despite this, the State seems hopelessly bogged down in any efforts to make life easy for distillers. As of January 2016, there were only three craft distillers in Georgia. Prior to this bill, a craft distiller could not sell a bottle to a patron at his tasting room. This Bill now allows the craft distiller to charge a fee for a distillery tour. As part of the fee, the patron gets to take home a 750 ml bottle of spirits. Clearly Georgia still has a long way to go.

Hawaii: Hawaii Revised Statures, Chapter 16 section 281 govern craft distilling in the State. A craft distiller with a valid Class 1 Manufacturing License can sell his product to licensed wholesalers. A craft distiller may further sell his product to retail customers at his distillery provided the alcohol is made from Hawaiian grown agricultural produce. However, no alcohol will be consumed at that location without additional approvals from the State.

Idaho: in mid-2014, Idaho took a big step forward with State Bill 1335. This Bill allows Idaho distilleries to provide samples of their products at their manufacturing facilities provided the samples offered are free; offered on the premises of the manufacturer's distillery site, limited to one-quarter ounce and only given to people in three sample quantities over a 24-hour period. Prior to this legislative change, visitors to Idaho distilleries could view the distilling process, but they could not taste or consume any of the spirits. Craft distillers in Idaho will fall under the purview of the Idaho State Liquor Division and Idaho Statutes Title 23. The legislation appears rather tame with no glaring roadblocks. Of course, this is the state level. Individual counties in the state might take a different view towards craft distilling. As of January 2016 there were about six craft distillers in Idaho. State taxes are $10.92 per gallon.

Illinois: Illinois Compiled Statutes, Chapter 235, section 5 provides for craft distillers to have a Class 9 License which will allow for sales to distributors. The fee for the license is $1800. A craft distiller license shall allow the manufacture of up to 35,000 gallons of spirits by distillation per year. A craft distiller licensee may sell such spirits to distributors in the State and up to 2,500 gallons of such spirits to non-licensees (ie the general public) in a face to face manner at the craft distillery. State liquor tax is $8.55 per gallon. At the beginning of 2016 there were 10 craft distillers in Illinois.

Indiana: laws in Indiana are a bit complex as far as I can see. Indiana Code Title 7.1, Article 3, section 7 allows for a person to be granted a permit for the commercial manufacture of alcohol. House Bill 1283 passed in 2013 allows for a craft distilling license under which a craft distiller can make up to 10,000 gallons of product per year. However, the applicant for a craft distiller permit must already have held a distillers permit for three years preceding the application for the craft permit. A craft distiller can make the product, sell it to wholesalers and even offer samples at a tasting room. If you are in Indiana, you will have to get legal advice on the issue of apparently having to have a distillers permit prior to applying for the craft permit. State tax on liquor in Indiana is $2.68 per gallon. At the beginning of 2016 there were two craft distillers in the State.

Iowa: in Iowa, Code 123.43(A) allows for the manufacture of distilled spirits to sell to the Iowa Alcoholic Beverages Division, with the option of sampling and selling bottles at the manufacturing location. At the beginning of 2016, there were only a handful of craft distillers in Iowa. State liquor tax in Iowa is a steep $12.43 per gallon.

Kansas: this was the first state in the Union to outlaw alcohol during Prohibition times. 2012 House Bill 2689 which became effective July 1, 2012 paved the way for craft distilling in the state. The overall application process for a craft distillers license is governed by the Kansas Department of Revenue. In many ways, the application process looks like something out of the Prohibitin era. From making detailed disclosure as to who owns the furniture at the distillery to how much you have in your various bank accounts, Kansas appears to be a tough nut to crack. There are very few craft distillers in Kansas – and I can see why.

Kentucky: Kentucky Revised Statutes 243.120 governs craft distilling. A craft distiller in Kentucky can make up to 50,000 gallons of product a year and can sell from his or her souvenir shop/tasting bar. Samples, not to exceed one ounce in size can be given to customers. No customer can buy more than three gallons per day. Hours of operation of a distillery shall be 9am to 9pm, Monday through Saturday. State tax on liquor is $6.76 per gallon. At the beginning of 2016 there were about a dozen craft distillers in Kentucky.

Lousiana: Louisiana Laws Title 26 governs alcohol. The State Alcohol and Tobacco Control department takes care of all the practicalities of alcohol manufacture. Steps involved in getting approvals include:

1.Obtain the appropriate surety bond from the Louisiana Department of Revenue. Please contact the Department of Revenue (225)219-7656.

2. Register Product Labels online, view information at http://www.atc.la.gov/productlabeling

3. Complete Louisiana Application www.atc.la.gov
a. Permit fees ($1000).
b. Schedule A and Fingerprints.
c. Attach a copy of a bonafide lease or proof of ownership of the premises to be licensed.
d. Attach a copy of all corporate documentation and proof of registration and good standing with
the Louisiana Secretary of State.
e. Attach proof of lease or ownership of delivery equipment.
f. Attach proof of contract or agreement with at least one alcoholic beverage distributor.
g. Attach a diagram of the premises to be licensed.
h. Attach an in-depth description of the business model that clearly describes the production process and equipment utilized.

4. Obtain a local alcoholic beverage manufacturer permit (parish or city).

5. Obtain all required occupational and health licenses (state and local).

6. Ensure that bottle sizes and packaging comply with state requirements.

At the beginning of 2016, there were only eight craft distillers in the State. Perhaps this onerous application process has something to do with this?

Maine: Maine Revised Statutes, Title 28A, part 1355 governs small batch distilling. A craft distiller must not make more than 50,000 gallons of product a year. A craft distiller can apply to have up to two off-site retail locations where product will be sold. Craft distillers must distribute their alcohol through the State Government. Craft distillers making less than 25,000 gallons can make application to sell their product to the public from their craft distillery. State tax on liquor in Maine is $5.80 per gallon.

Maryland: Maryland Code g2b-2-202 allows for an applicant to receive a Class 1 Manufacturing License which allows for the making of up to 27,500 gallons per year of brandy, rum, whiskey or alcohol and neutral spirits. A craft distiller can offer tours of his location, provide samples (not more than three) in one-half ounce sizes and sell up to three standard 750 ml bottles to a patron. Forgoing this right to sell bottles from the craft distillery will allow the distiller to produce more than 27,500 gallons annually. The annual license fee in Maryland is $2000. State alcohol tax in Maryland is $4.41 per gallon.

Massachusetts: in this State, Title 20, Chapter 138 governs alcohol production along with the Alcohol Beverages Control Commission. Each city has a Licencing Board that oversees alcohol permits. There is a designation in this state for a Farmer-Distiller license authorizing producing, manufacturing or distilling of distilled spirits by a person who grows fruits, flowers, herbs, vegetables, cereal grains or hops for the purpose of producing alcoholic beverages. A farmer-distillery may sell at wholesale to licensed farmer-distilleries, manufacturers, wholesalers, and licensed retailers in Massachusetts, at wholesale to other buyers specified in state law, and at retail by the bottle for consumption off the premises. A Manufacturer of All Alcoholic Beverages License is a license authorizing the manufacturing, rectifying or blending of all kinds of alcoholic beverages and sale of those beverages manufactured, rectified or blended to other licensed manufacturers, wholesalers and retailers in the State. Liquor tax in the State is $4.05 per gallon. At the beginning of 2016 there were about ten craft distillers in the State. For more details please see http://www.mass.gov/abcc.htm.

Michigan: the Michigan Liquor Control Commission oversees craft distilling in the State. A Small Distiller license is a:

License issued by the Liquor Control Commission to manufacture spirits, not to exceed 60,000 gallons annually of all brands combined. This License also includes the manufacture of Brandy. A craft distiller may offer free samples to consumers on the manufacturing premises. The craft distiller may sell spirits to consumers for consumption on the manufacturing premises.
The craft distiller may sell spirits to consumers for off-premises consumption (take-out) for not less than the uniform price set by the Commission. The craft distiller may not sell spirits directly to Michigan retail licensees. The craft distiller may sell spirits to the Michigan Liquor Control Commission who resells spirit products through the spirit distribution system.

Minnesota: this is another state that is slowly easing away from the Prohibition-era mentality. In mid-2015, legislative changes finally made it possible to sell bottles of product direct to the customer. The maximum production allowable for craft distillers is 40,000 gallons. A fee of $2000 and a surety bond of $3000 must be paid when applying for a craft distilling license. A separate license will be required if serving cocktails at your distillery.

See http://mn.gov/elicense/licenses/licensedetail.jsp?URI=tcm:29-53377&CT_URI=tcm:29-117-32 for details. State tax on alcohol in the state is $8.71 per gallon.

Mississippi: Title 67, Chapter 1, section 51 allows for the granting of an alcohol manufacturing license. There were two craft distillers in the state as at the start of 2016 and alcohol tax is $7.41 per gallon. The Office of Alcohol Beverage Control (ABC) oversees alcohol permits. The annual permit fee is $4500. There are 38 counties in the state that are dry. Do your homework carefully – it appears that this state is not overly open to distilling.

Missouri: there are about 10 craft distillers in the state as at the end of 2015. Missouri Revised Statutes Chapter 311, section 180 is the prevailing legislation. A tax bond ($1000 or so) will be required at the time of your license application. State liquor tax is $2 per gallon. Missouri actually allows for home distillation. Revised Statutes 311.055 states: No person at least twenty-one years of age shall be required to obtain a license to manufacture intoxicating liquor, as defined in section 311.020, for personal or family use. The aggregate amount of intoxicating liquor manufactured per household shall not exceed two hundred gallons per calendar year if there are two or more persons over the age of twenty-one years in such household, or one hundred gallons per calendar year if there is only one person over the age of twenty-one years in such household.

Now that's what I call progress!

Montana: the Montana Department of Revenue Liquor Control Division will oversee the application process. See http://revenue.mt.gov/Portals/9/liquor/alcohol_beveragelicenses/licensing_forms/MDLA.pdf for the application process. The maximum annual output in the state is 25,000 gallons. State liquor tax is $9.34 per gallon.

Nebraska: the State Liquor Control Commission oversees alcohol manufacture. State alcohol tax is $3.75 a gallon. At the start of 2016 there were six craft distillers in the state. Annual output is capped at 10,000 gallons. Sections 53-101 to 53-1,122 of the Nebraska Statutes govern alcohol.

Nevada: in 2013, Nevada took its first steps away from Prohibition era thinking with the passage of Assembly Bill 153. This bill makes allowance for a craft distiller to sell 10,000 cases in-state per year and 20,000 cases out of state per year with a case being 12 x 750 mls. State Assembly Bill 186 is currently winding its way through the system and it will provide for further relaxations including an increase to the two bottles per person per month limit and an increase to the two ounces total that can be sampled at a tasting room. There are at present a handful of craft distillers in the State. As laws are relaxed, that number will rise. State alcohol tax is $3.60 per gallon.

New Hampshire: Title 13, Chapter 178 of the NH Statutes govern alcohol in conjunction with the NH Liquor Commission. Craft distillers can sell at their facility only up to 3000 cases (nine liters per case) per year. There were seven craft distillers in the state at the end of 2015. There is no state liquor tax.

New Jersey: The department of Law and Public Safety – Alcohol Beverage Control Division governs alcohol production. The craft distilling license fee is about $1000. A similar sized bond must also be submitted. Annual outout is capped at 20,000 gallons. State liquor tax is $5.50 per gallon. The lengthy application form can be found at this link: http://www.nj.gov/oag/abc/downloads/Craft-Distillery-License-Package.pdf.

New Mexico: The NM Alcohol and Gaming Division oversees craft distiller applications. NM Statutes Chapter 60, Article 6A provides craft distilling details. A minimum of 1000 gallons per year must be made by a craft distiller. State liquor tax is $6.00 per gallon. At the end of 2015, there were six craft distillers operating in the State.

New York: the State of New York had over 60 craft distillers at the start of 2016. The New York alcoholic beverage control law has revolutionized craft distilling in the state. A class A-1 license will allow for the making of up to 35,000 gallons per year which can be sold to a liquor wholesaler. A class C license will allow a craft distiller to make only fruit brandy. A class D license will allow for the making of alcohol from agricultural products. This is the category that has fueled the explosive growth of craft distilling in the state. State liquor tax is $6.44 a gallon.

North Carolina: the State Alcohol Beverage Control Commission governs permits for alcohol manufacture. NC Statures Chapter 18B is the legislation. I cannot find any notation as to the maximum allowable annual production. At the start of 2016, there were nearly 25 craft distillers in operation. State liquor tax is $12.36 a gallon. Distillers must sell product to a wholesaler. Liquor prices are subject to an 80 % government markup at retail locations.

North Dakota: Title 5, Chapter 1, Section 19 of the North Dakota Century Code governs craft distilling. A craft distiller may sell to retail patrons at the distillery location. All other sales must be through wholesalers. The one quirk with North Dakota is that at least 51% of the ingredients, excluding water, used by a craft distiller to create distilled alcohol must be North Dakota grown agricultural products. State liquor tax is $4.66 a gallon.

Ohio: State liquor tax in Ohio is $9.32 per gallon. At the end of 2015, there were just over 20 craft distillers in the state. The Ohio Department of Commerce Division of Liquor Control will handle the application process for a fee. A craft distiller will want to get an A-3-a permit which will allow for the annual making of up to 10,000 gallons. You cannot serve more than four, quarter-ounce tastings per day to a person and that person cannot buy more than 1.5 liters of product from you per day.

Oklahoma: Title 37, section 518 (the Oklahoma Alcoholic Beverage Control Act) provides for the issuance of a manufacturing license with an annual fee of $3150. State alcohol tax is $5.56 per gallon. This appears to be a very difficult state. Obtain legal advice before getting in too deep. At the start of 2016, there were only a couple distilleries in the State.

Oregon: Lots of action here with over 40 craft distillers in business at the start of 2016. State tax, however, is a big $22.73 per gallon. http://www.oregon.gov/OLCC/pages/craft_distilleries.aspx provides you with the details of getting started in this friendly state.

Pennsylvania: at the start of 2016, there were close to 25 craft distillers operating in this state. Liquor tax is $7.21 per gallon. The state Liquor Control Board has an application for application for license. manufacture, storage or transportation of alcohol. The annual limit is 100,000 gallons.

Rhode Island: at the start of 2016, there were only a couple distillers in the state. Liquor tax is a modest $3.75 per liter. The annual license fee is $3000. A $5000 bond must accompany your application. The following link will take you to the application form http://www.dbr.ri.gov/documents/divisions/commlicensing/liquor/LQ-Instructions-Application-Ind-Ptnrship.pdf.

Title 3, Chapter 6 of the Rhode Island statutes govern alcohol production. The Department of Business Regulation controls alcohol sales and distribution.

South Carolina: at the start of 2016, there were just shy of 20 craft distillers operating in the State. State liquor tax is $5.42 per gallon. State law defines a micro-distiller as one who makes less than 125,000 cases of product per year. Tasting can be given to patrons, but only up to 1.5 ounces per day. Hours of operation are restricted to between 9am and 7 pm. Bottles sold at the distillery must be priced similar to retail prices at other locations in the county. The bi-annual fee for a distillery is $5000. Sub-article 11, Article 3, Chapter 6, Title 6 of State Code governs craft distilling.

South Dakota: Chapter 35, section 13 of the State Code governs craft distillers. 50,000 gallons is the allowed for annual production. State liquor tax is $4.68 a gallon. The one quirk of this state is the provision that at least 30 % of the raw materials, other than water, used by an artisan distiller to produce distilled spirits shall consist of agricultural products grown in South Dakota. At the start of 2016, there were a half-dozen craft distillers in the State.

Tennessee: the Tennessee Alcohol Beverage Commission administers distillation. See the information at the following website: https://www.tn.gov/abc/topic/distillery-license. At the start of 2016 there were about 20 craft distillers operating in the state.

Texas: at the beginning of 2016, there were about 40 craft distillers in Texas. State liquor tax is a modest $2.40 per gallon. The Texas Alcohol Beverage Commission (TABC) will grant a Distillers and Rectifiers Permit. You will also need a Manufacturers Warehouse License. The guidelines for all of this can be found at https://www.tabc.state.tx.us/publications/licensing/GuideWholesalers.pdf. There will also be a label approval process to navigate through.

Utah: alcohol is not condoned by a large portion of residents. Also, state liquor tax is $12.19 per gallon. This may explain why there are only six distillers in the State. The application fee is $3800 and the annual renewal fee is $2900. A surety bond of $10,000 is also required. Title 32B, Chapter 11 of State Statutes govern alcohol production. For more information, visit the following link: http://abc.utah.gov/license/licenses_manufacturing.html.

Vermont: At the start of 2016 there were about 15 craft distillers in Vermont. State alcohol tax is $5.86 per gallon. The website http://liquorcontrol.vermont.gov/licensing/instructions provides further details. Distillers can offer tastings and sales at Farmer's Markets and also at their distilleries under a 4th Class License.

Virginia: At the end of 2015 there were about 20 craft distillers in Virginia. State alcohol tax is a big $19.19 per gallon. Fees for licenses are on a sliding scale based on production volume: ≤ 5000 gallons annually: $450, 5001–36000 gallons annually: $2,500, ≥ 36,001 gallons annually: $3,725. The Virginia Department of Alcohol and Beverage Control in Richmond will handle the entire licensing process.

Washington: at the start of 2016, there were over 65 distilleries in the state. State alcohol tax is a huge $35.22 a gallon. The Washington State Liquor and Cannabis Board is the governing body overseeing craft distilling. Regulations say: For distillers who are producing 150,000 gallons or less of spirits per calendar year, at least half of the raw materials used in the production must be grown in Washington.

A distiller may sell spirits of its own production directly to a consumer for off-premises consumption, provided that the sale occurs when the customer is physically present on the licensed premises. A sample of .05 ounces is permitted with a maximum of two ounces per person per day. A distiller may also sell spirits of its own production to licensed Washington State Spirits Distributors and Spirits Retailers. A distiller may maintain an approved warehouse off the distillery premises for the distribution of spirits of its own production.

West Virginia: at the start of 2016 there were about nine distillers in the State. One license category is that of mini-distiller. Annual output is capped at 10,000 gallons and 25 % of the raw materials used must be grown or produced on-site. You cannot sell more than 3000 gallons in the initial two years of being licensed.

The other category of license is that of a distiller. Similar requirements apply as to output within the first two years. West Virginia further uses something called the Bailment Process where you must submit 10 % of gross sales to the Government each month who in turn will share these proceeds pro-rata with other spirits retailers in your area. Outdated and backwards to be sure. Think carefully before venturing into West Virginia.

Wisconsin: at the start of 2016 there were about 18 distillers in Wisconsin. Chapter 125 of the State Statutes offers details on permits. A craft distiller will need a manufacturer permit which will authorize the manufacture, tasting and retail sale of product.

Wyoming: at the start of 2016, there were but a handful of craft distillers in Wyoming. There are no state alcohol taxes in Wyoming. The Wyoming department of Revenue, Liquor Division is the body granting licenses. Title 12, Chapter 2 legislation in Wyoming appears restrictive, going so far as to limit a patron to no more than two tasting samples a day. Think carefully before deciding to set up in Wyoming.

In addition to state requirements, craft distillers in America will also have to obtain Federal approvals.

At the Federal level, a craft distiller must obtain a Distilled Spirits Plant Permit, commonly called the DSP permit. TTB form F 5110.41 and form F 5110.25 must be filed as part of obtaining a DSP permit.

The Federal Government wants assurance that it will receive taxes due on any spirits made by distillers. Accordingly, craft distillers will have to obtain a surety bond and file TTB form F 5110.56. Think of a surety bond as an insurance policy. In the event Washington fails to receive taxes due on your alcohol produced, it will simply collect on the insurance policy. Washington also wants to know who is making alcohol. TTB form F 5000.9 must be completed and full disclosure made as to who you are and who your partners (if any) are. Washington is further interested in learning about the effect your craft distillery will have on the environment. TTB form F 5000.29 must be submitted with environmental details. You may be further asked to submit form F 5000.30 that outlines water quality considerations. Do not be surprised if you are asked to provide information on the nature of any spent grain effluent to be discharged. The Clean Water Act is coming into play for craft distillers (and brewers too) in that Governments are becoming alert to BOD and COD levels. These test levels are a measure of how much organic material is present in your effluent. Organic matter that might damage the ecological viability of sewage settling ponds and treatment facilities.

Had enough yet? To round things out, you may be asked for a copy of your floor plan, a description of equipment to be used, a description of your process, an indication of how much alcohol will be made and a description of the security measures at your building.

LABELLING, CODES & ZONING

Labelling – Canada: In Canada there is little government interference with labels. A craft distiller can design his or her own labels and not have to waste any time seeking approvals. Government agencies do however reserve the right to conduct spot checks to determine label conformity to laws. For example, the minimum font size shall be 1.6 mm based on the lower cased letter 'o'. The bottle volume and %age alcohol must be clearly stated. The name and address of the distiller must also be stated. So long as the spirit falls under one of the standard definitions, no other requirements apply. However, a distiller making a spirit from sugar beets, for example, would not be able to call the product a Rum. A distiller making a Moonshine would have to make label disclosure that the spirit was made from grains as there is no standard definition in Canada for Moonshine. In my experience, government agencies in Canada are helpful when it comes to questions on labelling.

Labelling – America: the following URL will take you to a TTB label brochure - http://www.ttb.gov/pdf/brochures/p51902.pdf . In America, a distiller will be granted a Certificate of Label Approval (COLA) for the label that will appear on his or her bottle. In many cases, individual States will also want the distiller to submit copies of approved labels. Federal Statute 25 CFR Chapter 5 contains all the details concerning Labelling of Spirits. Look up this legislation on-line and settle in for a lengthy read.

Codes – Canada: A craft distiller in Canada wishing to start up will have to get Fire Inspection approvals. The Fire Inspector will lean heavily on the National Fire Code and its designations of F1 (high hazard) and F2 (medium hazard) for distilleries. Different inspectors will interpret the Code in different manners. It is critical to note that the Fire Inspector has absolute total discretion. He (or she) can make your start-up easy or they can turn your life upside down. It is thus critical to retain the services of an architect or a mechanical engineer who is intimately aware of the F1 and F2 ratings as applied to distilleries. Have that person do the talking for you. Get wrapped up in a dispute with the Fire Inspector and you may never see your distillery dream come true. Issues that will enter into the equation include: having a suitable fire wall between the distilling area and the tasting room area, having the boiler in a separate room complete with various safety shut-down devices, having explosion proof lighting, having incendiary proof electrical junction boxes, having suitable burn ratings on walls between your distillery and a neighboring business and maybe even having your grain grinding area isolated to a separate room. Building Code approvals will also be required. Expect to go down the path of having to have proper ventilation and air flow in your distillery. City or Municipal approvals will too be required. Expect to hear from officials on matters such as number of parking stalls at your distillery. Expect to have detailed discussions on the nature of effluent materials you will flush down the drain. Expect to have to provide data on expected BOD and COD levels. Expect to have to engage a testing lab to assess the biological nature of spent grain and waste stillage liquids from a typical still. These test levels are a measure of how much organic material is present in your effluent. Organic matter that might damage the ecological viability of sewage settling ponds and treatment facilities.

Codes – America: A similar scenario will play out in America where the NFPA Code will rear its head. Again, advisable to hire an architect or engineer to assist you in getting Fire Inspector approvals. The primary concern of the Inspector will be explosion and fire. It is likely that alcohol will be regarded as a Class 1 B liquid. If your distillery exceeds a certain square footage (possibly 12,000 square feet), expect the expensive topic of sprinkler systems to arise. NFPA 61 governs combustible dust. Expect to have discussions regarding locating your grain grinding activity to a separate, ventilated room. Building Codes and Electrical Codes will come under close scrutiny as well. Building inspectors may zero in on the subject of ventilation for your space. Electrical inspectors will focus on explosion proof lighting, junctions and panels. The International Mechanical Code, section 1004 covers boilers. Expect to have to locate your boiler in its own separate room and expect to have to outfit the boiler will various safety shut-off controls. The other code entanglement you may face is that of OSHA. If you are planning to hire any employees, you will likely have to come into compliance with all manner of safety requirements, safety meetings and protective equipment.

Zoning: not all parts of towns and cities are zoned for alcohol manufacture. When contemplating a distillery, it is essential that you first meet with members of your local Planning or Zoning Committee. Explain to them what you are wishing to establish. If they are unsure as to exactly what parts of your town are alcohol zoned, solicit the help of an architect who understands the zoning peculiarities of your town or city. If a re-zoning is required, expect the process to take far longer and to be far more frustrating than you ever imagined. I am aware of a craft distiller in Canada who encountered lengthy delays when a member of the public simply questioned whether or not a craft distillery will generate any black mold similar to what is common at the big bourbon distilleries in Kentucky.

Codes – UK: In the UK, you will run into several special requirements. Authorities will likely ask for a DSEAR (Dangerous Substances and Explosive Atmosphere Requirements) evaluation to be completed for your proposed distillery location. You may be required to undertake a HAZOP (Hazardous Operation) study of your planned facility. You may also have to complete an ALARP (As Low As Reasonably Possible) risk analysis study for your location. Another risk analysis study that you may have to complete is a LOPA (Layers Of Protection Analysis) study. If contemplating a craft distillery in the UK it is wise to seek the opinion of an engineer or architect well versed in these studies.

14

BUSINESS PLANNING

It is likely that at some stage of the approvals process you will be asked to submit a Business Plan to the regulatory authorities. If you are seeking bank financing or private investor financing, then you will certainly need a Business Plan. If you are partnering with others to create a craft distillery, a Business Plan can also help you to clarify who brings what to the table and who is responsible for what.

Search on-line and you will find books on Business Planning and likely templates to follow as well. Your banker may have a standard Business Planning template to share with you. What follows in this chapter is a suggested format of how to construct your Business Plan.

Executive Summary: the front part of your plan should contain a tightly written executive Summary that sums up the entire plan in a few paragraphs.

Confidentiality: include a detachable sheet in your plan that can be signed. Build in some standard confidentiality agreement wording. The last thing you want is for a curious investor to take a copy of your Plan and use it to build his own craft distillery.

Company Description: in a paragraph, describe your craft distillery and who you are.

Company Profile: in a paragraph, outline the name, address of your distillery and a description of the key players in your venture.

Mission Statement: describe what exactly your craft distillery is setting out to do. This statement will go a long way towards convincing the reader of your plan to invest in your distillery. What problems are you seeking to solve? How will your distillery make the world of distilled spirits better?

Vision Statement: what will the distillery's future look like as it starts to achieve its mission and goals?

Strengths and Weaknesses of your Distillery: what are the particular strengths of your planned distillery business? What are the weaknesses? Be honest with yourself as you list and describe these. Every business has weaknesses that will need to be mitigated.

Products: in detail, describe the products you plan to make at your distillery.

Strengths and Weaknesses of your Products: what are the strengths and weaknesses of your planned products?

Industry Analysis: describe in detail what has been happening in the distilled spirits market for the past number of years. Describe how craft distilling is impacting the distilled spirits market. What trends do you see emerging? How will your products fit in with these trends? This is a difficult section to complete. Visit your local library and do a literature search through old magazines and periodicals. Talk to people in the liquor distribution business. Gather data from places like the American Distilling Institute and visit distilling conferences and events.

Who is Your Target Market? To assist you in identifying your ideal buyers, check with your local city administrators for demographic data for your city. There are also data mining firms that can sell you demographic and customer habit data for specified geographic regions. Speak with your Chamber of Commerce about your planned distillery. Speak to local bartenders and mixologists about what you are planning. Arrange some focus groups to get a feel for how people view distilled spirits. Keep gathering data until you have a firm understanding of your target market.

Pricing: how will you price your products? What are the Government liquor taxes or markups? How are the big brand name products priced?

Competition Analysis: how many craft distillers are in your Province or in your State? Provide significant detail on all of them. Obtain their products and do some sampling with family and friends. Report these sampling observations in your plan. Make sure you intimately understand what competing products are on the marketplace.

Strengths, Weaknesses, Opportunities, Threats (SWOT) Analysis: undertake a complete SWOT analysis at this point incorporating everything you have discussed in your Business Plan so far.

Marketing Plan: how will you market and sell your product? How will you draw a crowd to your tasting room?

Operational Details: who will be responsible for what at your distillery? Who will your suppliers be? Where will your operation be located? What are the details of your lease agreement for your location? Who will your bank be? What will be your hours of operation? What invoicing and accounting procedures will you adopt? What will your audit procedures be? What about your month end reporting procedures? What insurance policy coverage will you need? Cover it all.

Regulations: describe in detail what province, state and county government regulations you must abide by. Describe also the building, electrical and fire codes you must adhere to.

Funds and Uses: detail how much money you will need to start up. What pieces of equipment must you buy. Provide a spreadsheet detailing projected inflow and outflow of cash for three years into the future.

15

FINAL THOUGHTS

This book has covered a lot of ground in a short number of pages. Starting a craft distillery is by no means an easy task, as I am sure this book has reminded you. But, don't let a bit of hard work stop you. The consumer out there is demanding unique spirit drinks made in unique ways. And that consumer is demanding more of it.

Home distilling can be quite an adventure in itself, from designing your own recipes, making your own heads, hearts and tails cuts, to proofing your own distillate and even to aging it in oak. Say good-bye to the big commercial brands. Chart your own course.

Whether you want to become a home distiller or whether you want to launch a small craft distillery, a fascinating journey awaits you.

Bon Voyage and Cheers!

16

GLOASSARY OF TERMS

Acetobacter: bacteria that converts ethanol to acetic acid.

Aerobic: with or in the presence of Oxygen.

Al-Ambic Still: a still design dating to 620 AD comprising a pot and am onion-shaped upper portion. Used today for production of spirits such as Cognac, Armagnac and brandy.

Aleurone Layer: the outer layer in a grain kernel where enzymes are synthesized.

Alpha-Amylase: an enzyme synthesized in a grain kernel. Hydrolizes the bonds alpha 1,4 between glucose molecules.

Alpha 1,4; the bond responsible for creating linear chains of starch.

Alpha 1,6: the bond responsible for creating branched chains of starch.

Amylose: a linear chain of starch.

Amyloglucosidase: an enzyme capable of breaking alpha 1,6 bonds.

Amylopectin: a branched chain of starch.

Anaerobic: without Oxygen.

ATP: a free energy compound generated during the EMP process.

Azeotropic Point: the mixture ratio of two liquids such that boiling the mixture will not cause further purification.

Beta-Amylase: an enzyme synthesized in a grain kernel. Hydrolyzes the bonds alpha 1,6 between glucose molecules.

Budding: the process by which Saccharomyces Cerevisiae yeast cells reproduce.

Cellulose: an extremely long chain of glucose molecules. Cellulose is a main constituent of wood.

Crabtree Effect: the ability of yeast to stop consuming Oxygen and start consuming sugar.

Cytoplasm: the interior structure of a yeast cell.

Distillation: The separation of two miscible liquids by virtue of differences in their respective boiling points.

Embryo: that part of a grain kernel that generates a root and a shoot.

EMP: Embden Meyerhof Parnas metabolic pathway responsible for the conversion of glucose into alcohols.

Endosperm: the interior of a grain kernel.

Enzyme: a protein substance that acts as a catalyst for a chemical process.

Fructose: a saccharide molecule of structure $C_6H_{12}O_6$.

Gay Lussac: French scientist, mid 1800s, who advanced the understanding of fermentation.

Gelatinization Point: that temperature where the structural integrity of a grain kernel breaks down.

Giberellin: hormone responsible for generation of enzymes in a grain kernel.

Glucan: gummy protein substance responsible for containing starch molecules in a grain kernel.

Gluconobacter: a member of the acetic acid family of bacteria. Causes fruit to spoil.

Glucose: a saccharide molecule also of structure $C_6H_{12.}$

Grist: grain that has been passed through a roller mill or hammer mill.

Hemicellulose: a very long chain of modified glucose molecules. A main constituent of wood.

Invertase: an enzyme generated by yeast through protein synthesis to aid the yeast cell in absorbing maltose and maltotriose.

Klyveromyces Maxianus: a strain of yeast used to ferment lactose in the production of Alpha Vodka.

Lactobacillus: bacteria commonly found in cheeses, yogurts and sourdough bread.

Lactone: cyclic esters of hydroxycarboxylic acids. Typically present in toasted and charred oak wood.

Lactose: a saccharide formed by the combination of a glucose and a galactose molecule. Used in the production of alcohol for Alpha Vodka.

Leuconostoc Meserenteriodes: a high alcohol tolerant bacteria.

Lignin: a complex organic polymer found in the structure of wood.

Maltose: two glucose units joined together.

Maltotriose: three glucose units joined together.

Malting: the process in which grain kernels are sprouted.

Mashing: the process in which grain is taken to above its gelatinization temperature to liberate starch molecules and break down the structure of the kernel.

Mitochondrion: that part within a yeast cell where self-replicating DNA material is stored.

Molasses: the industry term assigned to the sludge residue remaining after sugar has been extracted from cane juice.

NADH: a free energy compound generated during the EMP process.

Nucleus: that part within a yeast cell where DNA and protein material is stored.

Pectin: a natural polysaccharide occurring in fruits, when heated it causes thickening. A precursor to methanol formation in fruit spirits.

Pomace: the mixture of seeds and skin left after pressing grapes.

Protease: an enzyme generated by yeast through protein synthesis to aid the yeast cell in absorbing maltose and maltotriose.

Pyruvate: a key intermediate product in the metabolic conversion of glucose to alcohol.

Raoult: French scientist, mid 1800s, who advanced the understanding of distillation.

Ribosomes: that part of a yeast cell where proteins are synthesized.

Saccharomyces Cerevisiae: the dominant species of yeast used in brewing and distilling.

Sour Mash: a technique involving the use of stillage in a subsequent grain mash.

Starch: a combination of multiple glucose molecules.

Stillage: the liquid remaining in a still after the completion of a distillation run.

Sucrose: a saccharide molecule formed by the combination of a glucose and a fructose molecule.

Surface Tension: the elastic tendency of liquids that makes them acquire the least surface area possible.

Tannin: naturally occurring polyphenol found in plants, seeds, bark, wood, leaves and fruit skins.

Vacuole: that part of a yeast cell acting as a storehouse of nutrients.

Vapor Pressure: pressure exerted by a vapor in thermodynamic equilibrium with its condensed phases (solid or liquid) at a given temperature in a closed system.

Zymomonas Molbilis: a waterborne bacteria noted for imparting funky aromas as it consumes sugar.

17

ABOUT THE AUTHOR

Malcolm Bucholtz, is a graduate of Queen's University Faculty of Engineering in Canada and Heriot Watt University in Edinburgh, Scotland. After graduating from Queen's University in 1986, he embarked on a career in the steel industry. With his first paycheque in hand he went to a local home brewing store where he bought Charlie Papazian's book, *The Joy of Home Brewing* along with all the tools and toys needed for making beer at home. Although not realized at the time this purchase would have lasting and profound implications.

In 1999, Malcolm completed his MBA from the Edinburgh Business School at Heriot Watt University. This opened the door to exciting opportunities over the next 15 years in the financial brokerage industry as well as the junior mining industry. During this time, Malcolm started making beer using the all-grain method, wine from fruit and a delightful beverage called mead.

In early 2014, Malcolm began yearning for new adventures. While contemplating the idea of returning to Heriot Watt University to pursue a graduate degree in Fermentation Science, he happened upon the U.K.-based Institute for Brewing and Distilling (IBD) and enrolled to write their General Certificate Exam in Distilling. Popular rumors have it that Malcolm may have purchased an al-Ambic pot still and a Hillbilly column still to assist him with his studies. To this day he will neither confirm nor deny these rumors.

In late 2014, Malcolm began delivering 5-day Distilling Workshops at Urban Distilleries in Kelowna, British Columbia, Canada. When not delivering workshops, Malcolm offers his consulting services to entrepreneurs seeking to launch small craft distilleries. Assistance in crafting business plans and marketing plans plus assistance with recipe development and operational start-ups are just a part of what he offers.

You can find Malcolm at his website, www.ProhibitionUniversity.com.

Find him on Facebook at his Prohibition University page and follow him on Twitter @ProhibitionU.

18

DISTILLERY WORKSHOPS

If you have developed a burning passion to get involved in small batch distilling, whether as a craft distiller or as a home distiller, you may be interested in gaining more knowledge through attending one of my 5-Day Distillery Workshops. The basic format of a Workshop is as follows:

Day 1: starts with a colorful review of the History of Alcohol interspersed with various samplings and critical analysis of commercially produced spirits that the Canadian/American consumer is accustomed to seeing on the shelf. As a craft distiller, one must be cognizant of these products and their shortcomings if one is to create and market a product that will compete for the consumer's attention. As a home distiller, these tastings might inspire you to create unique recipes.

You will be engaged in a study of the legal definitions of spirit types in Canada and the USA as set down by Canadian Food and Drug Regulations and/or the American Alcohol Tax and Trade Bureau. This study will be interspersed with more spirits sampling and critical analysis.

A good part of Day 1 will also see you enjoy plenty of floor time in the distillery to study the layout of a working distillery and the various pieces of equipment needed for successful distillery operation.

Day 2: starts with a detailed study of grains and other raw materials available to craft distillers and home distillers, as well as a detailed study of the grain malting process.

You will then participate in mashing a small batch of grain to observe how the natural enzymes in malted grain convert the starches to sugars. This will be followed by the making of a small batch of grain mash using artificial enzymes to illustrate the ease of using these man-made enzymes.

During these small scale mashes, you will be treated to a practical introduction to some of the tools that a craft distiller will use to analyze a mash.

You will then learn about the nasty bacteria that can cause problems to a distiller and you will be introduced to the various sanitizing chemicals that a distiller can use to combat bacteria.

This classroom work will be followed by hands-on grinding of some grain and the making of a full-size mash in the distillery.

Back in the classroom, we will examine water, yeast and the science behind the fermentation process.

We will then engage in an in-depth discussion of the various botanicals that a craft distiller can use in making Gin.

Day 2 will conclude with a chance to enjoy more floor time in the distillery to further study and evaluate the layout of a working distillery and the various pieces of equipment needed for successful distillery operation.

Day 3: the success of any craft distillery will rest in large part on its ability to reach out to the consumer and market its craft distilled creations. There is much more to marketing than just running a few ads here and there. Marketing is a science unto itself. On day 3, you will delve deep into the science of marketing including an exercise in critiquing and analyzing other craft distillers' websites. This in-depth study of marketing will be interspersed with more samplings and critical analysis of various craft distilled spirits. This in-depth study will also be interspersed with a chance to participate in the creation of a small batch of Gin on a small 10 liter Copper al-Ambic pot still.

Day 4: the mathematics and physics of the distillation process at first glance appear complex. But, distillation is easily understandable and this portion of the workshop will ensure that you fully understand the process.

To put your distillation knowledge to work, you will engage in hands-on participation of filling a still with a fermented mash. Then, under the guidance of the Master Distiller, the class will work together to conduct a stripping run. You will make the heads and tails cuts and taste and smell the heads, hearts and the tails. The spent mash from this distillation run will be pumped from the still and time permitting the class will re-load the still and conduct a second stripping run.

As a craft distiller or a home distiller, you will have to proof your spirits down to a suitable alcoholic strength. You will be introduced to the Canadian Excise Tables / American TTB Proofing Tables and will practice using them by engaging in some hands-on proofing exercises.

As a craft distiller or a home distiller, you may want to mature your distilled spirits in oak barrels. We will delve into the science of oak barrel manufacture and oak barrel aging.

Day 5: Bottle filling, packaging and labelling is a vital part of the craft distilling process. On day 5, you will explore the various options available to a craft distiller for caps, bottles and labels. Some jurisdictions require governmental approval of labels. You will be introduced to this protocol.

Every province / state regards craft distilling in a different legislative light. You will explore the various requirements of the different provinces / states. This will be complimented with a discussion of Surety Bond requirements.

You will critically analyze the structure of a business plan and will be shown how the 4-P's of marketing can be properly used in a Business Plan.

You will be shown you how to prepare the financial projections for your planned craft distilling operation so you can determine your needed equipment sizes and capabilities.

More floor time with the Master Distiller will be made available throughout this final day so you can ask any final questions.

I am now contemplating starting to offer 2 and 3 day variants of these curriculum. If you have a craft distillery and are interested in hosting Workshops, please contact me. I would enjoy hearing from you.

I have now also developed the format for a 1-day Gin Master Class. Each class starts with a review of the various botanicals used to make Gin. Touch them, feel them, smell them, taste them. Next, participants are introduced to small bottles of alcohol in which various botanicals have been steeped. Using a small flask containing 50 mls of juniper infused alcohol, participants build their own Gin by adding measured drops of the various samples of botanically infused alcohols. This exercise is designed to show how the taste profile of a Gin can be easily manipulated with just a few drops of something. Based on this experience, participants then collaborate as a class to define two Gin recipes. Participants measure and weigh out their chosen botanicals which get added to some alcohol in an Alembic still. Participants then tend to the still to conduct the distillation runs. Using the Canada Excise Tables, participants then work as a group to proof their newly made Gins to the best tasting alcoholic strength. The day concludes with everyone taking home small bottles of their Gin creations.